Gardening

Organic Vegetable Gardening Made Easy

By Ace McCloud
Copyright © 2016

Disclaimer

The information provided in this book is designed to provide helpful information on the subjects discussed. This book is not meant to be used, nor should it be used, to diagnose or treat any medical condition. For diagnosis or treatment of any medical problem, consult your own physician. The publisher and author are not responsible for any specific health or allergy needs that may require medical supervision and are not liable for any damages or negative consequences from any treatment, action, application or preparation, to any person reading or following the information in this book. Any references included are provided for informational purposes only. Readers should be aware that any websites or links listed in this book may change.

Table of Contents

Introduction 6
Chapter 1: Build Your Own Organic Garden................ 8
Chapter 4: Select Your Vegetables 20
Chapter 5: Tools For an Incredible Garden 26
Chapter 6: Planting Seeds 31
Chapter 7: Care and Feeding Of Organic Gardens 52
Chapter 8: Harvesting Your Vegetables 65
Chapter 9: Delicious Vegetarian Recipes 69
Conclusion..76
My Other Books and Audio Books............................... 77

Be sure to check out my website for all my Books and Audio books.

www.AcesEbooks.com

Introduction

I want to thank you and congratulate you for buying the book, "Gardening: Organic Vegetable Gardening Made Easy."

If you are tired of driving and then paying for poor quality produce and are looking for easy ways to grow your own healthy and fresh food while saving money, then this is the book for you! Vegetables are some of the healthiest foods around, providing us with many key vitamins, minerals and nutrients. These include calcium, fiber, folate, iron, magnesium, potassium, sodium, Vitamin A, Vitamin C and more. In fact, many people have documented a variety incredible health benefits from switching to a mainly vegetable diet. If I were to list all of the fantastic claims over the last fifty years it would take up the next 100 pages!

Vegetables are a staple ingredient in many recipes and can provide endless delicious and healthy dining options for you and your family. While you're probably used to purchasing vegetables at a local supermarket, where you can easily just pick them up, wash them, and cook them, what if I told you there is a much better way to acquire your vegetables, a way that is more economical as well as greatly beneficial to your physical and mental health?

The vegetables you buy at the supermarket are commercially grown, meaning that they are lower in nutrients than organically grown vegetables. In addition, they are usually treated with chemical pesticides, which can leave a harmful residue on the skins. Commercially grown vegetables are especially low in magnesium, which is important for diabetes prevention, managing your blood pressure and cholesterol, and promoting a healthy heart.

Organically grown vegetables, which you can produce yourself in the comfort of your own backyard, are higher in nutrients and you can ensure that they are not subjected to harmful chemicals. Many people report that organically grown vegetables taste a thousand times better than what they buy at the store.

To grow your own organic vegetables, you will need to create a garden. Gardening is a great outdoor activity that can promote your physical and mental strength, while giving you ultimate control over what you grow and how you grow it. Gardening activities can complement strength training and cardiovascular exercise regimens. They have also been shown to help relieve mental stress and help stabilize the emotions.

Gardening can be very economical. One research study showed that planting a garden in your backyard can save you significant amounts of money. Although you will need to pay out a little for materials, the amount you'll save by not purchasing over-priced vegetables at the store will quickly show up in your budget.

Your garden can be as small as a window box or as large as a huge yard. Its format can range from a plot of land to an array of raised-bed gardens, to some pots on a deck or balcony. No matter the size, proper gardening can yield as much as a year's worth of vegetables to use for yourself or to share with friends and family. Just think of it! A year's worth of vegetables to use both immediately and in the future. When you grow your own food, you can choose to use it while it's fresh or you can store it for later use.

This book contains proven steps and strategies on how to create a perfectly sized, well-planned vegetable garden that will provide you with healthy versions of your favorite vegetables to enjoy pretty much year-round.

In this book you will discover in great detail how to plan your garden. I will describe how to pick the best spot to plant your garden, how to prepare the best soil, how to create your own organic compost, how to decide which vegetables to grow, and also how to determine which ones you can plant together. I will also explain how to plant each kind of vegetable, step by step, in the easiest method possible. You will learn proven organic methods to ward off and treat for specific garden pests and other conditions. You will discover the best time to harvest your garden and how to learn how to store any leftover vegetables. Finally, this book gives you some of the most delicious, healthy, and easy-to-prepare recipes that you can try out yourself using your own freshly grown vegetables.

Chapter 1: Build Your Own Organic Garden

Long before you place the first seed in your well-prepared soil, you'll need to decide what kind of garden you will plant. In this chapter we will discuss the four most popular formats for vegetable gardening.

You can easily start out with a small garden and eventually work your way up to a raised bed garden, which is the largest type of home garden. Here you will learn a little bit about each type of garden as well as the supplies you'll need and their approximate costs.

Container Gardens

Container gardens are small and inexpensive. You can easily grow vegetables in a container when you have limited space in your yard. Container gardens are popular among apartment dwellers and individuals with limited or no yard space. They are also a good option if you want to start small, if you are beginning to experiment with gardening, or you have a small budget.

The main advantages of container gardening are that they don't require extensive setup and they are inexpensive, utilizing materials that shouldn't cost more than $10 each. The only disadvantage of container gardening is that containers don't allow much room for root growth, so you won't be able to grow root vegetables.

To build a container garden, you will need:

- One or more containers, depending on what you plan to grow. A container should be at least 12 inches wide and 12 inches deep.

- Soil, either store-bought or from the ground.

- A small hand rake

- Seeds

- A water source

- Compost (optional, for plants that are heavy feeders)

Unfortunately, container gardens cannot accommodate all vegetables due to their size. However you do have quite few options. Container gardens can accommodate carrots, cucumbers, lettuce, green beans, zucchini, peppers, potatoes, and tomatoes. Since carrots grow well with lettuce, tomatoes, and peppers, you may want to select a combination of these vegetables to grow together. Since zucchini is a heavy feeder and its long vines can suffocate other plants, it is best grown in a separate container with lots of compost for food.

Window Box Gardens

Window box gardens are even smaller than container gardens but are great when you have extremely limited space. A window box garden can also be a great first attempt when you're learning how to manage plants, since it is so small and inexpensive to set up. The greatest advantage of a window box garden is that it is small, easily manageable, and is easily accessible from any window of your house. Just make sure the window you choose gets plenty of sun exposure! The primary disadvantage of a window box garden is that its minimal depth limits the kind of vegetables you can grow.

To build a window box garden, you will need:

- A window box
- Soil, either store-bought or directly from the ground
- Seeds
- A water source, such as a watering can

Leafy green vegetables such as lettuce and spinach are the best plants to grow in this type of garden since they have shallow roots. You can also grow herb plants. While it is possible to grow carrots and tomatoes in a window box, you'll want to ensure that your box is much deeper than standard size.

In-Ground Garden

This is the most common type of garden, especially for beginners. All you need is about 500 to 600 square feet and your garden can produce ample vegetables for fresh eating and storage. You can easily create an in-ground garden in your backyard as long as you have the room. The advantage of an in-ground garden is that it is large enough to accommodate multiple vegetables while being pretty easy to manage. The disadvantages are that they require a little more effort and money than container and window box gardens and they are more susceptible to pests.

To build an in-ground garden, you will need:

- Soil, as found or in the ground of your garden space, although you can truck in additional soil as needed to fill in low spots or supplement nutrients
- Fencing material (can range from a simple barricade of bricks to chicken wire)

- A hand tiller

- Seeds

- Compost

- Stakes or trellises, if planting climbing varieties

- A watering system

You may also choose to include some of the extras you will learn about throughout this book, such as netting and other protection.

When it comes to choosing what plants to grow together in an in-ground garden, the choice is up to you, based on which vegetables grow well together. One benefit to an in-ground garden is that you can divide it up into multiple, small garden plots that cater to the specific needs of different plants. For example, most plants in the cabbage family can be planted with herbs, potatoes and onions, all of which can be turned into a healthy meal. Beans, lettuce and potatoes have the most compatibility combinations. While onions and peppers often grow well on a plot together, spinach is usually best left to grow by itself.

You won't go far wrong if you utilize the garden planning practices you will discover throughout this book Pay attention to what grows well together and which plants have similar soil requirements, when grouping your vegetables and laying out your garden.

Raised Bed Gardens

These are the most complex form of gardening, but they are great for large areas and can usually result in large yields. If you choose to purchase store-bought beds, premade for your convenience, you may find yourself spending a little more. However, you can easily save money if you are willing to build the beds yourself.

The advantages of a raised bed garden are that you can more easily grow the most varieties, the soil warms quicker because it is closer to the sun, and it offers great soil drainage. The primary disadvantage of a raised bed garden is that it will take you a little longer to design and put together than any of the other gardens in this chapter.

To build a raised bed garden, you will need:

- Wooden boards (cedar is the best because it doesn't rot)

- Topsoil

- A hand tiller
- Seeds
- Water
- Compost

To create the frame, cut your wood to the size you want (two by six is a good size for beginners), fit them together and use a drill to screw them together securely. Once you've built the frame it is important to set it evenly on your gardening soil to prevent drainage problems. Next, you will add soil to the bed. Pour in topsoil mixed with compost to get a high quality of material for growing your vegetables.

While you can grow any combination of vegetables in a raised bed, certain plants fare better than others. Pumpkins grow especially well in raised beds, since they are such heavy feeders and their vines can become massive in size. Many gardeners have also had success with beans, broccoli, brussel sprouts and spinach.

Chapter 2: Pick a Spot For Your Garden

The first step to creating a vegetable garden is to decide where you will plant it. The location of your garden is a very important factor because if you don't plant it in an ideal location, your garden can end up dying out or barely producing, so all of your hard work will go to waste. Some factors you should consider in picking a garden spot are exposure to sunlight, soil quality, drainage, and access to water. You may find that you need to plant multiple gardens, based on the needs of specific vegetables and the lay of your land. I will teach you the exact requirements for planting a thriving, healthy garden.

Proximity

People commonly plant a garden in their backyard because they can easily access it every day. You could also start a garden in your front yard or in an easily accessible public area such as a community park or school, just as long as you get the proper permission.

Wherever you choose to plant your garden, you should make sure you can easily bring in supplies such as mulch, compost, and water. It should also be located near a source of water. Lugging a watering can back and forth or having to drag a hose all around your property can quickly become annoying, not to mention exhausting.

How Big?

If you are new to gardening, it is best to start small. A good-sized beginner's garden should start at about 100 square feet; over time, you can build it up from there. If you plant too large of a garden on your first try, you may find it overwhelming to maintain.

If your objective is eventually to have a garden where you can grow, store and share vegetables, then I suggest you work toward a size of 600 square feet. This is the perfect size for a fully functioning vegetable garden.

Go For Flat And Sunny

The terrain for your garden should be flat. Planting on a slight south-facing slope is acceptable, because this will give your garden more sunlight exposure in the spring. However, too much of a slope can cause soil erosion that robs your plants of valuable nutrients. Planting a garden at the bottom of a hill or in a ditch will probably result in drainage problems. It is best to ensure that your garden is slightly elevated.

If at all possible, select the location for your garden in the Fall. That way, you have plenty of time to gather your resources, prepare the soil, and plan your planting layout, in short – so you will be ready to act, come spring.

One important factor to consider in your plan is the placement of trees around your garden. Planting too close to a tree could lead to two problems: too much shade and too many roots in one place. Your garden should ideally be situated in a large, open area where the sun can freely shine down on it. Even if your garden area is sunny in the midsummer, it could easily be blocked by blooming trees and shadows from nearby objects in fall and early spring.

Vegetables generally require about six hours of direct sunlight to grow properly. Tomatoes, beans, peppers, cucumbers, squash and eggplant need a full six hours of sunlight. Leafy vegetables such as lettuce and spinach usually need only three to four hours of direct sunlight to grow properly. Root vegetables like carrots and potatoes can benefit from six hours of sunlight but will grow well with a little less direct light.

The sunlight doesn't have to be constant. For example, if your garden requires six hours of sunlight but gets only two hours of sun exposure in the morning, three in the late afternoon and one in the evening, it would still receive a total of six hours of direct sunlight. Since different type of vegetables require different amounts of sunlight, it is common for gardeners to have multiple garden spots around the yard, based on available sunlight. If you live in a climate where winters are mild, it is possible to garden year-round. You only need to ensure that your garden area receives adequate sunlight during all seasons.

Here's one way to determine whether your chosen garden spot will have adequate sun exposure. Stand in the garden and face southward. Extend your left hand eastward and your right hand westward. Move your left hand along the southern sky until it is behind the horizon in the west. If there is nothing in the way to block the light then you've got yourself the perfect spot. You can also place wooden stakes in the ground and monitor how long the sun casts a shadow over them to determine how sunny that location will be.

Ensure Adequate Drainage

Drainage is essential to the success of your garden. Vegetable roots do not like being wet all the time; they tend to rot. The area for your garden must be well-drained.

When you are evaluating the amount of sunlight for a garden spot, also watch for standing water when it rains. Avoid creating a garden in a spot if the area floods after a rain shower and the water stands there for more than 10 minutes.

Another way to check for adequate drainage is to dig a small hole, about three to five inches wide and at least 8 to 10 inches deep. Pour water into the hole until it is full. If the water completely soaks into the soil in 15 minutes or less, the soil is well-drained.

Some backyards tend to be a little soggy. If that is the case, create raised beds in the highest part of the back yard. Prepare the area and place about two inches of gravel at the bottom. This will filter water out away from the soil and the roots of your plants. Place soil atop the gravel.

Map It Out

One useful strategy for preparing your garden is to map it out before you plant. Now that you have picked a potential garden spot, draw a sketch of it. You can then mark areas that are too low or too high, the areas with the greatest and least sun exposure, drainage concerns, and other considerations. You can then map out where you will plant each type of vegetable. Mapping out your garden can save you a lot of time and hassle and you can jump right into gardening as soon as the season arrives.

Soil Conditions

Finally, you should evaluate the quality of the soil throughout your chosen garden spot. The soil for a garden should ideally be loose and rich. The looser the soil, the easier it will be for your vegetables to grow roots. You'll also want to consider the depth of the soil. Many first-time gardeners believe they only need six to eight inches of depth but the truth is that plants and vegetables will need more room than that to grow properly. An ideal depth is 12 to 18 inches of prepared soil.

You can add nutrients to fertilize the soil and prepare it to nourish your vegetables. You have the choice of using store-bought chemicals, even organic fertilizer from the store, or you can apply your own organic fertilizer, such as grass clippings or vegetable remains. Organic fertilizer is usually preferred, because it can provide a higher amount of natural nutrients.

The quality of your soil, and the process of preparing it for planting, is important enough that I've devoted the next chapter to a more thorough discussion of soil preparation.

Chapter 3: Soil Preparation

Outside of sun exposure, the quality of your soil is the single greatest influence on the productivity of your garden. If you plant in bad soil or soil that is not optimized for gardening you will most likely end up with low to no yield. Building up your soil is the best way to ensure that you can guarantee a plenty of healthy vegetables. This chapter will teach you effective strategies to easily prepare your soil so you can get the most out of your garden.

The soil in your backyard may not be suitable in its current condition for growing vegetables. It may need some improvement. Soil for organic gardening is full of good things like compost, good bacteria, and minerals. Compost consists of decaying matter that adds everything your organic vegetables need to grow.

If your vegetables grow well, they are less likely to attract bugs and disease. Three of the most important minerals a garden needs are potassium, nitrogen and phosphorus. Your garden soil requires an abundance of these three minerals because vegetables need them in large quantities to stay healthy and grow. These are called primary nutrients. What we call secondary nutrients – sulfur, magnesium and calcium – are also important.

Another issue is the type of soil you have. Some backyards come equipped with fluffy, air-filled soil. In most cases, however, the soil is impacted, full of clay or sand, and hard as a rock. Imagine being a tomato plant and trying to push your roots through that! Additives like compost, peat moss, manure and mulch help to transform a clay-like soil into a texture more friendly to gardening. The same additives can also change sandy soil into something that holds water long enough to nourish your plants.

The Advantage of Raised Beds

The best way to build up soil is to create raised beds. Raised beds provide sunlight, drain easily, promote good air circulation, allow for more planting space and are easy to maintain. To easily make a raised bed, till the soil you're working with, add organic nutrients, and mound it into a bed. Since the soil in raised beds is often loose and rich, it may yield four times the results of non-raised beds. Research shows that raised beds make for more efficient planting. They save you in weeding time because the plants grow closer together, so they block out other weeds.

Because raised beds have hard sides that prevent soil from slipping out into the yard, it is possible to fill them with organic potting soil. This soil comes in bags and is often sold at garden centers. It is the best soil in which to grow organic vegetables because it is already rich and aerated. You need do nothing except plant in it. The only problems with organic potting soil are that you cannot walk on this type of soil, because you do not want it to be compacted and, because it is so light, you may have to add a layer of mulch on top to keep the soil from blowing away in a high wind.

The shape of your raised bed can make a huge difference in your yield. You should round the tops of your beds to get the best results. Raised beds with an arc at the top can provide room for more vegetables to grow. Your yield should increase roughly by 20% for each rounded top. You can also plant leafy vegetables such as spinach and lettuce around the edges of the bed to make even more growing room.

If you're going to grow vegetables that have variations in their sunlight requirements then it is best to create multiple beds. Planting multiple beds is highly efficient because you can rotate the vegetables each year, which will promote their growth.

Balance Your Soil's pH

The first step in getting your garden ready for planting is to start preparing the soil. You can do this either in the fall or the spring. The soil is most easily managed in the spring. The best way to determine the quality of your soil is to perform a pH test. Soil pH testers are inexpensive and are easily found in most garden supply stores. The ideal pH level for good soil is neutral, as indicated by the number 7 on testing materials.

If the soil reads low (2 to 5), you can add agricultural lime to balance its acidity. The best time to add lime is in the fall, letting it set all winter and then digging it into the ground in the spring. Lime requires some time to change the soil composition.

If the pH level reads too high, you can add gardener's sulfur or organic nutrients in the form of compost, combined with acidic additives such as pine needles. Another useful method to check the texture is to grab some soil in your hand and roll it up into a ball. If you drop the ball from chest level and it breaks apart when it hits the ground, the soil is ready.

Till the Ground

Once you've cleared an area, the next step is to strip the grass and the first layer of soil from the surface of the ground. Using a spade or other helpful digging tool, you can then dig twelve to eighteen inches down. Get rid of foreign objects or anything that will not belong in your garden such as weeds, rocks and debris. Using a pitchfork is more effective than a shovel to remove rocks and other debris. This is because the forks can penetrate the soil better and catch any foreign matter without losing any soil. Another useful method of digging out the area for your garden is to use a garden tiller.

Loosen the soil in the garden area and then add three to four inches of nutrients to the ground in the form of compost, manure, fertilizer or organic elements such as eggshells or peanut shells. After you've added everything, dig it in, using a shovel or garden tiller to about 12 inches and rake the soil until it is even.

Aerating the soil promotes root growth and will boost the earthworm population. You can also aerate the soil by gently digging into it with a fork. You can add peat or coir to help maintain the texture of the soil. To best maintain the soil throughout the season and during the fall, spread half an inch of compost over the soil when the bed is empty and gently dig the top two inches with a fork. You should refrain from walking on the soil as to not disturb it. The best way to avoid this is to shape your beds narrow enough that you can reach them from your walkway.

Add Organic Matter to Soil

I've mentioned several times that adding organic matter to your soil can help promote good soil and a high yield of vegetables. This section will provide an in-depth look at adding organic matter to your soil to get the best results. The best way to add this matter to your soil is to dig the first six inches, especially for young crops, as the organic matter will easily reach the roots. The best sources of organic material include:

1. **Compost** – Compost is chock-full of nutrients that promote crop growth and soil vitality. Many gardeners keep a sealed compost bin near their vegetable garden. Composting is great for the environment because it enables you to recycle kitchen waste, contribute less to landfills, and it serves as a natural fertilizer with no chemicals. Here is a list of some things you can add to your compost:

    - Table scraps (mix with leaves or other dry carbon item)
    - Fruit/vegetable remains (mix with leave or other dry carbon item)
    - Crushed eggshell
    - Shredded leaves
    - Grass clippings
    - Shrub prunings
    - Straw or hay
    - Pine needles

- Flowers
- Seaweed or kelp
- Ashes from wood fires
- Coffee grounds
- Tea leaves
- Black and white newspaper
- Shredded cardboard
- Wood chips

Additionally, you can add store-bought soil to the compost to help dilute any bad odors that come out of your compost bin. Never add meat, bones, fish, weeds or diseased plants into your compost, or you may attract pests. Because fruit peels may be covered in pesticides, they should be avoided as well.

You can purchase plastic compost bins at your local garden center. They look much like a trash can but have holes in the side to allow air to enter. Other, more expensive types consist of a rolling cylinder (looking like a BINGO ball roller) with a handle that lets you roll it every so often.

Build your own compost bin in your backyard near the garden using untreated wood or old fashioned chicken wire. Use wood to build a three-sided box that is about two feet high and as wide as you like. The front is open so that you can easily access the compost. Another way to make a compost pile is to place heavy duty stakes in a large circle and tie 2-foot high chicken wire to them. Overlap the wire at the ends to make an entryway and start piling in the compost materials.

Composting Process

To begin the composting process, you'll want to start with bare earth. This enables organisms to naturally aerate the compost and they will eventually be moved to your garden bed. Laying straw or twigs first can help create excellent drainage. Begin to add your compost materials in thin layers, switching between moist and dry items. Sprinkle materials such as wood chips or ash thinly so they do not clump together. Next, add in manure or any other material that will give off nitrogen to activate the compost pile. You should always keep your pile moist, whether by watering it yourself or by letting the rainwater it for you. Covering the pile with wood or plastic will help lock in heat and moisture.

Use a pitchfork and turn the pile every couple of weeks to aerate it. At this point, you can add new items by simply mixing them in instead of adding them in layers. Some composting bins rotate themselves to make the turning process easier. Finally, aim for a balance of carbon and nitrogen in your compost to keep it healthy and balanced. A great compost pile contains more carbon than nitrogen. An easy way to make sure you attain this proportion is to use one-third green items to two-thirds brown items.

2. **Manure** – Aged manure from cows or horses is a good source of organic material. When using animal manure, the only thing you need to be aware of is the possibility of weed seeds germinating in the manure and harming your garden. However, you can easily reverse the effect of any weed seeds by combining the manure with mulch.

Chicken manure adds a great deal of nitrogen, phosphorus and potassium to the compost. However, it should never be applied directly to the garden because it can burn your plants. Rabbit droppings, sometimes referred to as pellets because of their appearance, are full of nitrogen and are very good for your garden. Alternatively, you can use green manure, which is made of chopped legume plants.

3. **Store-Bought Soil Amendments** – Most department stores and gardening centers will carry soil amendments you can buy, based on your individual gardening needs. Glacial rock dust is a popular amendment, as many gardeners use it to help replenish the minerals and nutrients leached from the soil after a year of gardening it.

Chapter 4: Select Your Vegetables

There are many different vegetables you can plant in your garden. Each vegetable has its own needs, in terms of sunlight exposure, water, fertilizer and a preferred soil pH for optimum production. In this chapter, you will learn a little bit about each type of vegetable to help you decide what you want to include in your garden.

You will also learn which vegetables you can plant together in order to boost your yields. This is called companion planting, which is a reliable method of organic gardening. Some plants enhance the growth of others and keep pests away as well.

Beans

Beans are a highly nutritional vegetable that contains fiber and can increase your body's resistance to certain diseases. Bean varieties range from green beans, to lima beans, butter beans and soybeans. Beans have a long history of cultivation and can be found in many home gardens today.

You can grow beans near beets (bush bean varieties only), any vegetables that fall in the cabbage family, carrots, celery, cucumber, corn, potatoes or radishes. Beans actually fix nitrogen in the soil, which enhances the growth of companion vegetables. At the same time, these other plants boost the development of beans, in a symbiotic relationship. Avoid planting beans near garlic and onions or you may stunt their growth.

Beets

Beets are root vegetables that are great for your heart. These roots contain antioxidants that are believed to protect you against coronary heart disease and strokes. Beets are also believed to have <u>anti-aging</u> properties. Beets grown in a home garden are low in calories and contain plenty of vitamins, minerals and fiber. The edible part is the root; therefore, nitrogen is not as important since it tends to enhance the green part of the plant.

You can grow beets near, onions, lettuce, garlic, and any vegetable that belongs to the cabbage family. Avoid planting beets near pole beans.

Broccoli

Broccoli, part of the cabbage family, is a green vegetable with a large flower of a head. It is a cool-weather crop, meaning it doesn't grow very well during hot summer temperatures. Broccoli is a great source of vitamins C and K. Homegrown broccoli has a low amount of carbs, as well as providing protein, fiber, and fat.

You can grow broccoli near beets, celery, lettuce, cucumbers, spinach, onions, and potatoes. Do not plant broccoli near tomatoes, which can stunt its growth.

Brussel Sprouts

Brussel sprouts are small leafy vegetables that look like tiny cabbages on a stalk. They contain plenty of Vitamin C, Vitamin K, B vitamins, minerals, and fiber.

You can plant brussel sprouts near beets, celery, lettuce, cucumbers, spinach, onions and potatoes. Avoid planting them near tomatoes to avoid growth stunting.

Cabbage

Cabbage is packed with antioxidants, Vitamin C and is low in fat. These antioxidants are believed to lower "bad" cholesterol and protect against breast, colon, and prostate cancers. Cabbage also contains plenty of Vitamins B5, B6, and B1. In terms of minerals, cabbage contains iron, magnesium, potassium and manganese.

You can plant cabbage near beets, celery, lettuce, cucumbers, spinach, garlic onions and potatoes. Avoid planting it near tomatoes to avoid growth stunting.

Carrots

Carrots are a root vegetable with high resistance to insects and diseases. Adding carrots to your diet can promote healthy skin and protect against aging, heart disease, and certain cancers including lung cancer. Carrots are loaded with vitamin A, which is great for your eyesight. Many herbalists believe that carrots can protect your body against infection. They may also protect your body against strokes and guard your dental health.

You can plant carrots near beans, peas, onions, lettuce, peppers, tomatoes and radishes. Avoid planting them near dill.

Cauliflower

Cauliflower is a flowering vegetable that is part of the cabbage family. It has been linked to cancer prevention and improved digestion and is good for your heart. Cauliflower is full of antioxidants that can improve your general health and promote anti-aging.

You can plant cauliflower near beets, celery, spinach, radishes, corn, and other members of the cabbage family. Avoid planting cauliflower near onions.

Celery

Celery is a low-calorie vegetable best known for helping reduce inflammation in joints and lungs. The magnesium in celery can help you relax and manage stress. Its fiber and liquid content make it very good for your digestive system. Like carrots, celery contains lots of Vitamin A, which can help your eyesight and protect against heart disease. Finally, research suggests that celery may help protect your body from pancreatic cancer.

You can plant celery near beans, tomatoes, and any other vegetable that belongs to the cabbage family. Avoid planting celery near garlic.

Corn

Corn is a classic but popular vegetable that contains Vitamins A, B, and E as well as important minerals such as magnesium, zinc, iron and manganese. Corn contains a high amount of fiber, which can promote a healthy digestive system and help reduce your risk of hemorrhoids and rectal cancer. Corn contains antioxidants that can protect your body from Alzheimer's disease. Additionally, corn can help prevent heart disease and anemia and lower your risk of broken bones and hypertension.

You can plant corn near cucumbers, beans, pumpkins, peas, radishes, potatoes and zucchini. Avoid planting it near tomatoes.

Cucumbers

Cucumbers are a delicious vegetable that have a climbing ability, making them easy to grow in almost any garden. Cucumbers contain Vitamins B and C. Since they are 95% water, cucumbers facilitate hydration. Their silicon and sulfur content can promote hair growth and reduce bad breath. Research suggests that cucumbers can help protect your body against breast, prostate and ovarian cancer.

You can also use cucumbers to aid you around the house. Rubbing a cucumber over a mirror can prevent fogging and rubbing it on a squeaky door hinge can erase the squeak. Additionally, eating a few cucumber slices before going to bed after a long night of drinking can reduce the effects of a hangover.

You can plant cucumbers near tomatoes, radishes, corn, beans, peas, and any vegetable that belongs to the cabbage family. Avoid planting near sage.

Lettuce

Lettuce is a great addition to a vegetable garden because home-grown varieties contain tons of vitamin A. Lettuce has few calories and no fat, but it has lots of cellulose and fiber, which can aid in weight loss. It also has high levels of Vitamin C and beta-carotene.

Among the many varieties of lettuce, each one has its own benefits. Romaine lettuce has high levels of omega-3 fatty acids and protein. A cup of kale provides your daily requirement of vitamins C, A and K, while giving you phyto-nutrients that fight cancer and heart disease. Spinach and Swiss chard contain significant amounts of calcium and iron. Interestingly, adding multiple types of lettuce to your diet can help you lower your risk of insomnia, boost your energy and help you think more clearly.

You can plant lettuce near beets, any member of the cabbage family, radishes, carrots, and onions.

Onions

Onions are easy to grow on raised beds. They can boost your immune system because they contain lots of Vitamin C. They also contain a high amount of chromium, which can help you manage your blood sugar. Many people believe that onions possess healing and anti-inflammatory properties. Slices of raw onion can help reduce the amount of bad cholesterol in your body. Finally, the bright green stems contain a significant amount of Vitamin A.

You can plant onions near beets, any member of the cabbage family, peppers, lettuce, carrots, and tomatoes. Avoid planting them near beans or peas because the onions will stunt their growth.

Parsnips

Parsnips are a vegetable with origins in Ancient Greece. They are often included in soup recipes. The two key nutrients in parsnips are potassium and folate, both of which promote heart health. Parsnips also contain high amounts of Vitamins C, E, and K as well as manganese.

You can plant them near beans, peas, onions, lettuce, peppers, tomatoes and radishes. Avoid planting them near dill.

Peas

Peas are an easy crop to grow. They come in three different varieties: sweet pea, snow pea and snap pea. Peas are an excellent addition to a garden because their roots add nitrogen to the soil, benefiting other crops. Peas are a great vegetable if you're looking to manage your weight, because they are low in fat but contain high amounts of all the healthy stuff your body needs, such as protein and fiber. Most significantly, peas contain a nutrient called coumestrol, which can protect your body against stomach cancer. Additionally, peas possess anti-aging properties, they can boost your immune system, and they are a great source of energy.

You can plant peas near corn, beans, carrots, radishes and cucumbers. Avoid planting them near garlic and onions.

Peppers

Peppers come in many shapes, sizes and colors and are a staple in most vegetable gardens. Bell peppers contain sulfur, which can protect your body against certain types of cancer. They also contain lots of Vitamin E, which slows the aging process. The B6 found in bell peppers can help boost your nervous system.

You can plant peppers near tomatoes, carrots and onions.

Potatoes

Potatoes are a versatile vegetable eaten in a variety of forms. Potatoes by themselves have few calories and tons of fiber, making them an excellent addition to a healthy diet. They contain plenty of vitamin B6, Vitamin C, potassium, phosphorous, copper and niacin. Additionally, potatoes contain antioxidants that can protect your body from heart disease. Research also suggests they can help lower your blood pressure.

You can plant potatoes near any member of the cabbage family, as well as near corn, beans, and peas. Avoid planting them near tomatoes.

Pumpkins

Pumpkins are a symbol of Fall, when they harvested, but their health benefits are useful all year long. They contain a large amount of Vitamin A, known to benefit the eyes. Many people don't know that pumpkins also contain a great deal of fiber. Eating a small amount of pumpkin with each meal can actually meet your day's fiber requirement. The seeds contain phytosterols which can help protect your body against bad cholesterol. The carotenoids found in pumpkins can prevent the skin from wrinkling and can help protect you against certain cancers.

You can plant pumpkins near corn or zucchini.

Radishes

Radishes have their roots – both literally and historically – in Southern Asia. They contain antioxidants that can help lower the levels of bad cholesterol in your body and thus protect you from heart disease. This root vegetable may protect your body against colon cancer. When you eat radishes, your body produces bile, which can help improve your digestion and treat constipation. Radishes also contain potassium, which can help moderate your blood pressure.

You can plant radishes near carrots, cucumbers, beans, peas, and lettuce.

Spinach

Spinach is a great vegetable that contains flavonoids, Vitamin C, Vitamin E, lots of fiber, and plenty of minerals and antioxidants. It that can protect against prostate cancer and is also known to have anti-inflammatory properties. Spinach can help you manage your blood pressure. It has also been reported to improve vision, boost the immune system and strengthen bones.

You can plant spinach near any member of the cabbage family.

Zucchini

Zucchini is a type of squash that is loaded with health benefits. It is packed with fiber and Vitamins C and A. Research suggests that zucchini possesses anti-inflammatory properties and can help protect the prostate. It is also high in manganese.

You can plant zucchini near corn or pumpkins.

Tomatoes

Tomatoes are a highly popular ingredient in pizzas, salads, sandwiches, and hamburgers, in addition to being delicious to eat by themselves. They contain Lycopene, an antioxidant that can prevent cancerous cells from appearing in your body. The nutrients in tomatoes promote healthy skin and healthy bones. They can help balance your blood sugar and improve your vision. Tomatoes contain Vitamin A and can even improve hair health.

You can plant tomatoes near peppers, carrots, garlic, onions, and leafy lettuce. Avoid planting them near potatoes, corn, or any member of the cabbage family.

The GrowVeg YouTube video, [How to Plan a Vegetable Garden: Design Your Best Garden Layout](#) provides tons of information on planning and growing different vegetables. It can serve as a useful additional resource for garden planning.

Chapter 5: Tools For an Incredible Garden

When you plant a garden you will need some special tools to help you build and grow the best garden possible. You can find many of the tools listed in this chapter at your local gardening or home improvement store or they can be easily purchased online. Gardening tools tend to be inexpensive. If you're just starting out, I would recommend opting for some of the simpler inexpensive equipment. You can always invest in more expensive and complicated tools as your savings grow and you gain more gardening experience.

Plant Sensors

Plant sensors are a fairly new technology that can especially benefit new gardeners. To use a plant sensor, all you need to do is stick it into the soil in an area you want to turn into your garden. You leave it for a few days, where it will collect data on sunlight, moisture, and other important factors that influence the health of your garden. One brand comes with a USB stick that you can plug into your computer after you've collected the data so you can compare it to their website to determine if your chosen area is the right spot for what you want to grow.

Seed Starter Pots

Seed starter pots, also known as cell trays or propagation containers, are multi-plant containers that enable gardeners to start seeds indoors. Seed starter pots are very useful if you live in a planting zone with a limited growing season or if weather conditions interfere with outdoor seed planting. They allow you to start plants well before the weather is conducive to outdoor gardening.

Seed starter pots are often made from biodegradable material that can be inserted directly into the ground. These biodegradable pots are usually made of peat. Alternatively, you can start seeds by putting potting soil in divided plastic trays. When the starts are ready to be planted outdoors, you simply pop them out of the tray and insert them into the prepared soil of your garden.

Tiller

A tiller is a useful powered machine that works garden soil until it's loose and broken up. It also facilitates mixing compost and other organic material into the soil. There are several types of tillers; choosing the best one usually depends on the condition of your soil as well as your own strength. Front-tine tillers have blades in front of the motor and require a great deal of strength to push through the soil. They are best for breaking up sod in new gardens and for maneuvering through rocky soil. Rear-tine tillers are good for tilling tight corners and rocky, hard soil. The downside of rear-tine tillers is that they are hard to control.

Spade

A spade is a helpful garden tool that serves multiple purposes. You can use it to dig up weeds, move soil, transport compost, and turn soil. Spades come in all different sizes and styles, the most popular being a small handheld spade. The type of spade you use will likely come down to your personal preference but the best way to choose a spade is to consider the size of the bowl, its sturdiness and its weight compared to your own.

Digging Fork

Digging forks often come with four long prongs that resemble a fork you eat with. Digging forks are best to use when you're doing a lot of heavy growing. They range from twelve-inch pronged tools to smaller varieties with shorter and narrower prongs, which make them useful for digging in tight spaces.

Trowel

Trowels are the ultimate digging tool. They are hand-held miniature shovels with short blades that come in multiple widths. Many gardeners use trowels to dig holes and create rows for planting seeds.

Wheelbarrow

Wheelbarrows are used to move around large quantities of soil, compost and other garden substances. They range in size and type, and your choice will depend upon your personal gardening needs. Wheelbarrows traditionally have only one wheel, located in the front, but some come with two or three wheels. As an alternative to the wheelbarrow, you may prefer a four-wheeled wagon.

Wheelbarrows can be heavy and difficult to maneuver with full loads so it's important to choose something you can safely handle. If you're not strong enough to lift and balance a single-wheeled wheelbarrow, you may want to opt for one with multiple wheels in front for added stability, or just choose a wagon.

Garden Rake

A level-headed garden rake with a straight back and sharp teeth is the best rake to have. You can use a garden rake for a multitude of tasks, including the breakdown and leveling of soil. You can also use either the teeth or the handle to create rows along which to plant your seeds. Garden rakes are usually made of sturdy metal with wooden handles.

Trellis

A trellis can be useful when working with climbing vegetables, to encourage them to grow upwards instead of sprawling out on the ground. By raising the plant off the ground, a trellis can help prevent vegetable rot.

Trellises are made from a variety materials and their use depends on what you're growing. Lightweight vegetables can grow on a trellis made of any material, but heavier vegetables require something strong enough to support their weight. Trellises are generally made of wire, wood, plastic, or metal. The only other consideration when choosing a trellis is your local climate. If your area gets a lot of rain, a wooden trellis will deteriorate faster than one made of metal or plastic.

Hoe

A hoe is another staple gardening tool that can serve multiple functions. You can use its flat blade to break up roots. You can use it to shift soil around, to create hills, and to dig trenches. Hoe blades are narrow enough to remove weeds between rows of vegetables.

Pruner

You can use a hand-held pruner to harvest vegetables and to prune back growth. There are three main types of pruners and the one you use will depend on your needs. Anvil pruners have a single sharp blade that cuts against a flat bracing surface. Bypass pruners have one or two sharp blades that work like scissors to make a close cut. Ratchet pruners utilize a ratcheting gear that increases your leverage. This type of pruner is a good choice for individuals with weak hands. Ratchet pruners are also designed for cutting heavier stems.

Netting

Netting is handy to have when you want to protect your vegetables from pests, such as birds and rats. Most netting is made of a nylon material and you can easily lay it right over your plants.

Cloches

Cloches are translucent, structures you can place over seedlings to protect them from inclement weather and creatures that would eat the tender shoots. At the same time, they allow sunlight in and vent air. Cloches come in several types of material. Plastic cloches are best for protecting crops row-by-row. Glass cloches are attractive and can properly insulate your vegetables but they are more likely to break than plastic ones. You can also make an individual cloche by cutting the bottom off a plastic soda bottle and placing it over a plant. The open top of the bottle provides perfect ventilation. Once the plants are established and the weather is friendlier, you can remove cloche coverage.

Harvest Basket

Harvest baskets are any type of basket that you use to store and transport your vegetables once you've picked them. I've used everything from laundry baskets to a wagon. You can also use harvest baskets to store and transport your tools to the garden, before you fill them with vegetables.

Rain Collection Barrel

Rain collection barrels can collect rain water for use in your garden. Using rain water to water your crops is a popular alternative to watering them with water from your garden hose, which can contain chlorine. Rain collection barrels come in various sizes but if you're just starting out with a new garden, a 50 gallon barrel will do the trick.

Watering Can

A watering can is used to transport small amounts of water to a small garden. It is especially useful for window boxes, hanging baskets and small plots that are isolated from a source of running water.

Sprinkler

A sprinkler is a useful tool when watering a medium to large-sized garden. Most sprinklers hook up to your garden hose; they are more portable than watering cans. They can also water a large piece of land in much less time than other methods. Another benefit of sprinklers is that you don't have to physically be there to water your garden – you can just set it up and walk away. Just remember to move the sprinkler or turn off the water before your ground becomes waterlogged.

Adjustable Hose Nozzle

Another watering option is to use an adjustable hose spray nozzle. The greatest benefit of using this nozzle is that it gives you complete control over how much water pressure you use. Many gardeners like to use the soft mist option for young plants and newly planted seeds with more intense settings for sturdy, well-established vegetables. A spray nozzle sure beats holding your thumb over the end of the hose!

Garden Sprayer

Garden sprayers are small to medium sized machines that will automatically spray out chemicals such as weed killer or bug repellant on your garden. Most weed killers come in small bottles with a sprayer attachment that mixes water from your hose, but many gardeners prefer to buy an individual sprayer and then hook it up to larger bottles of weed killer or nontoxic chemicals that can protect or nourish your garden.

Rain Gauge

A rain gauge will indicate how much moisture gets into your garden, either from natural sources (rain) or by supplementing with water from a hose or sprinkler. It is important that your vegetables get enough moisture in order to grow properly. A rain gauge can indicate when you need to supplement with water from your hose.

A simple rain gauge is a small tube with a ruler on it. It can be straight up and down or flair out at the top. A spike is situated on the bottom that is inserted into the soil of your garden. These gauges are made of plastic and will give you a good idea of how much moisture your garden is receiving.

Gardening Gloves

Gardening gloves are made from comfortable and rugged material that will protect your hands while you work in your garden. They are often made from cloth or leather and are sometimes water-resistant. Gloves can protect your hands from cuts, insects, calluses, dirt, splinters and germs. When you are not wearing your gloves, it is best to store them away from moisture and sunlight.

Gardening Apron

Gardening aprons are good to protect your clothes from getting dirty while you garden. They often come with pouches in the front that you can use to store small tools and seeds for easy access.

Gardening Journal

A gardening journal is an optional but powerful tool you can use to keep track of your garden's progress. You can write down what you've planted, what you've had success with, what failed to grow and any other important notes you may have. It is a good idea to keep track of crop rotations in your journal so you can refer back to them every year. If you're a beginner, I highly recommend keeping a journal for the first few years until you have a handle on everything and don't need to track it anymore.

Tool Storage

Consistent care of your gardening tools can help them last for years. When you're not using your tools, it is important to keep them stored in a dry place, usually your garage or basement, anywhere they will be safe from the weather. It is also important to clean, oil, and sharpen your tools regularly to keep them in the best working condition.

Chapter 6: Planting Seeds

You can't start a garden if you don't have any seeds. Sometimes the most direct way to obtain seeds is to take them directly from vegetables that are already grown. However, the most popular way of obtaining seeds is to buy them. The greatest advantage of purchasing seeds is that you can easily buy as many as you need. In addition, many store-bought seeds are bred to be resistant to disease. Another major benefit of store-bought seeds is the varieties you can find, all of which you will learn about in this chapter.

Certified Organic Seeds

If you are serious about organic gardening, you will want to buy certified organic seeds. They are a little more expensive, but you will be certain that they are non-genetically modified seeds. Organic seeds come from vegetables that were never subjected to manufactured chemicals. They have never been treated to stave off bacteria or to deter pests. The powder with which they are treated is a chemical. Organic seeds have not had their DNA tampered with as with genetically modified seeds. GMO seeds have been injected with a substance that changes their DNA. No one knows the long-term affects this will have on the vegetables themselves or those who eat them, hence the value of an organic garden.

Heirloom Seeds

Heirloom seeds are another option. These are seeds saved from vegetables that have come down through the generations. You can save your own seeds, but you need to be careful. Hybrid vegetables are made by combining different varieties of the same vegetable. A pink zucchini may have been created by breeding a purple zucchini with a white zucchini. Seeds saved from this hybrid can go back to either parent. The seed may produce a white or a purple zucchini, but the chances that a pink one will come out of it are very slim. You will have best results by saving seeds from organic or heirloom vegetables.

Beans

There are two primary types of bean. **Bush beans** grow in small bushes and are the easiest type of bean to grow. **Pole beans** are beans that grow as a vine and require some type of support system to allow them to grow upwards. Bush beans do not require any support structure and need only minimal care.

You should plant bush beans one inch deep and two to three inches apart in hills. You can also plant bush beans in rows but in this case you should space the seeds eighteen to twenty four inches apart. Once the seeds begin to form leaves, you can thin them to six inches apart. You can plant pole beans either in hills or in rows. They can go in the ground after putting the supports in the place. Pole beans require the same depth and spacing as bush beans. One advantage of growing a pole bean variety is that it gives you more vegetables for the space in your garden.

In general, once planted, you should water bean plants once a week – more if your area is experiencing dry conditions. Adding organic mulch or compost matter to bean plants can help lock in moisture and prevent the growth of weeds.

There are several types of bush and pole beans:

- **Green Beans**: Green beans are the most popular type of bean grown worldwide. This type of bean is not picky about its soil and can adapt to almost anything. Green beans also exist in both bush and pole varieties. Before you plant green beans you should work organic compost into the soil.

    Green beans are planted one inch deep. Bush beans are planted four to five inches apart while pole beans are planted six to eight inches apart. Rows of beans should be spaced thirty to thirty six inches apart. Once seedlings appear, you can thin them to between six and eight inches apart.

    You will want to water green beans so that their soil remains consistently moist. It is best to use aged compost for fertilizer.

- **Yellow Beans:** Yellow beans are similar to green beans but they only grow in the bush variety and they have a slightly different taste. To grow yellow beans, follow the same steps as for green beans.

- **Lima Beans/Butter Beans:** Butter beans are a form of lima bean with the same growing requirements of lima beans. They are flat and oval-shaped beans that grow in both pole and bush variety. Each type of bean has a unique flavor. You should plant lima beans three to four weeks after the last frost of the spring, if you didn't start them indoors, two to three weeks earlier.

    the bush type is planted one and a half to two inches deep, three to six feet apart in rows spaced twenty four to thirty inches apart. You should plant pole beans six to ten inches apart, in rows that are thirty to thirty six inches apart. Before you plant the seeds, you can work sand or vermiculite into the soil to help the seeds push through. Lima and butter beans can be watered regularly but it is important to monitor rainfall amounts to avoid overwatering.

- **Black-Eyed Peas:** This type of bean is commonly grown in the South due to its climate needs. The ideal soil temperature for black eyed peas is 65 degrees Fahrenheit. You should plant black-eyed peas in moist soil, one to one and a half inches deep, two to four inches apart, and in rows that are spaced two to three feet apart. Natural rainfall is a good enough watering source but if your area experiences little to no rainfall you can water them manually. Avoid using too much fertilizer as it can stunt growth.

- **Soybeans:** Soybeans grow on hairy plants that are tall and bushy. You can plant soybeans two to three weeks after the last frost of the spring. Soybeans require full sun exposure and the ideal soil temperature for planting is 60 degrees Fahrenheit.

  You should plant soybean seeds one to two inches deep and two to four inches apart. Rows of soybeans can be twenty four to thirty inches apart. Before you plant the seeds you can add aged compost to the soil to help promote growth. Once seedlings begin to appear you can thin them to six to eight inches apart. Water soybeans regularly, once pods and flowers begin to show. While pods are forming, they need around two inches of water each week. Weed carefully around soybean plants to avoid disturbing their roots.

Beets

The most commonly grown type of beet is the simple red beet but it comes in several varieties, which differ in days the crop takes to mature. Detroit dark red beets take 58 days, Early Wonders take 52 days, Sangria takes 56 days and Sweethearts take 58 days.

There are also a few hybrids with a variety of qualities. Avenger beets are best known for their round, green roots. Big Red beets are best for when you're planting late in the season. Gladiator beets take the least time to mature (48 days) and are good if you want to can them. Pacemaker beets have a 50 day maturity rate and produce great roots. Red Ace beets are best known to produce sweet roots in a short amount of time. Beets also come in a miniature version that is very tender.

The best time to begin planting beets is between three weeks before and after the last frost of the spring. Beets require full sun exposure although a bit of shade will not hurt them. The ideal soil temperature for growing this vegetable is 39 degrees Fahrenheit in loamy or sandy soil, although it is best to wait until the soil temperature reaches 50 degrees before planting. Beets require a soil pH of 6.2 to 6.8. Adding aged manure before you plant the seeds can help them germinate better. It also helps to clear the soil of rocks and any other debris that would impair the growth of the roots.

Beets have a mild tolerance to cold weather. They should be planted two inches apart and half an inch deep into the soil, in rows that are twelve to eighteen inches apart. Once seedlings appear, you can thin them to between one and three inches apart. It is best to fertilize beets at the same time you plant them and it is best to water them only during dry conditions. Too much nitrogen can damage the roots. It is best to plant beets in soil with a neutral pH to get a good yield.

This root needs plenty of phosphorous to grow full and delicious. Side dress with a little garden phosphorous once or twice during the growing season. To side dress, sprinkle some near the base of the plants and carefully scratch it into the ground, making sure to water well afterward. Keep the roots of the beet plant cool and moist by surrounding the plants with a layer of compost, straw, shredded bark or other organic mulch. If you live in an area with a low rate of precipitation, you can soak the seeds for one day prior to planting.

Broccoli

The main variety of broccoli is what you see in the supermarket, with its big, green heads. This type of broccoli is most commonly grown by commercial industries. However, there are several different varieties available for growth at home.

- **Sprouting Broccoli** – This type of broccoli develops shoots that many people use in stir fry dishes.

- **Broccoli Raab** – This type of broccoli branches out and develops several small heads instead of growing one big head.

- **Chinese Broccoli** – This type of broccoli is small in size. It develops dark green leaves and is rapid-growing. Its flavor is also different from traditional broccoli. Chinese broccoli is used in many Asian dishes.

The best time to begin planting broccoli is two to three weeks before the last frost of the spring. You can also start it indoors about six to eight weeks in advance of transfer to the garden. Broccoli requires full sun exposure and loose soil.

Broccoli seeds are best planted half an inch deep into the ground and twelve to twenty four inches apart in rows. Rows of broccoli should be planted thirty six inches apart. The ideal soil temperature for broccoli ranges between 55 and 75 degrees Fahrenheit, although it can grow in soil as low as 40 degrees. Aim for a pH of 6.0 to 6.8. It is best to add two inches of compost and a little bit of manure before you plant the seeds. Cover the ground beneath the broccoli plants with two inches of organic mulch to keep the roots cool.

Broccoli can withstand cold weather and it grows well in soil with a slightly acidic to a neutral pH. It is best to fertilize broccoli three weeks after you transfer the plant from indoor to outdoor conditions. Since it is a heavy feeder, you can add some calcium and magnesium to help promote growth.

You should water broccoli regularly and make sure it stays moist. However, you should avoid getting any developing heads wet when you provide water.

Brussel Sprouts

There are several hybrid varieties of brussel sprouts:

- **Confidant** – This type has a rapid maturity rate, is medium green in color and comes with a mild taste.

- **Genius or Cobus** – These take longer to mature and are best for planting late in the season. Since they are late season crops, these types tend to fare better in cold weather.

Brussel sprouts are another cool weather crop that should be grown early in the Spring or in early Fall. Actually, a light frost will greatly improve the flavor. The best time to begin planting this vegetable is indoors, six to eight weeks before the last frost of the spring. It is helpful to add rotted manure to the soil before you plant the seeds. You can water brussel sprouts as soon as you plant them.

The ideal soil temperature for brussel sprouts ranges between 55 to 75 degrees Fahrenheit in neutral soil. It is best to plant brussel sprouts on raised beds that are 12 to 24 inches apart. Brussel sprouts require full sun exposure and firm soil. Aim for a pH of 6.5 to 7.0.

Brussel sprouts can easily withstand cold weather. It is best to fertilize them three weeks after you convert them from indoor to outdoor conditions. You will also want to water them two to three weeks prior to harvesting.

Brussel sprouts enjoy nitrogen and will benefit from a top dressing of compost after they grow to about one foot high. The leaves of the plant will turn yellow as the Brussel sprouts are getting ready to be harvested. Don't mistake this for disease. Just remove the yellow leaves and discard them. You can use mulch to help this crop stay moist and cool.

Cabbage

Cabbage comes in five main varieties:

- **Green** – This type of cabbage is the one you most commonly see in the supermarket. It is green in color and sweet with tightly packed leaves.

- **Savoy** – This cabbage has ruffled and curly leaves. The leaves on these heads are more lose than traditional green cabbage.

- **Red** – This variety looks like green cabbage but is smaller and red in color. It is used in many German dishes.

- **Napa** – This type of cabbage doesn't come in a head but in long stalks with light green leaves. It looks similar to Romaine lettuce. Its flavor is mild with a slight twist of spice.

- **Bok Choy** – This type of cabbage grows in a stalk and appears similar to Swiss chard. It dons a sweet, mild flavor and is a popular cabbage for stir fry dishes.

The best time to begin planting cabbage is one week before to one week after the last frost of the spring. You can also plant them indoors six to eight weeks before planting outdoors. Cabbage can easily withstand cold weather.

Cabbage requires full sun exposure. Its ideal soil temperature is between 45 and 85 degrees Fahrenheit and it grows best in neutral loamy or neutral sandy, fertile soil. It is best to add compost or aged manure to the soil before you plant the seeds. Depending on how big you want the heads to grow, plant them between twelve and twenty four inches from each other. The closer the seeds, the smaller the heads will grow.

It is best to fertilize cabbage three weeks after you convert them from indoor to outdoor conditions. Give them two inches of water for two to three weeks prior to harvesting. Apply mulch thickly for this crop. Although cabbage is in the same family as broccoli and brussel sprouts, they all feed heavily off of the nutrients in the soil, so it is best to plant them away from each other to ensure each cabbage receives adequate nutrition.

Carrots

There are many types of carrot with wide variation in size, color and seed types. The most popular variety of carrots for home growers is the **Nantes carrot,** due to its ease of planting. Nantes carrots grow well in thick, rocky soil, unlike other varieties. There are several sub-varieties of Nantes carrots:

- **Scarlet Nantes** – A sweet variety that develops six to eight inches.

- **Bolero** – A cylinder-shaped variety that grows six to seven inches long and stays sweet well after harvesting.

- **Kaleidoscope** – This variety will grow in multiple colors including red, yellow, purple and orange. These carrots grow to a length of seven to eight inches.

- **White Satin** – This variety grows a white-colored carrot that develops up to eight inches in length.

- **Purple Dragon** – This variety grows a purple-colored carrot with an orange center. This carrot can grow to be between eight and ten inches long.

Carrots can easily withstand cold weather. The best time to begin planting them is three to five weeks before the last frost of the spring. Carrots require full sun exposure, although a little shade won't hurt them. Plant carrot seeds half an inch deep, half an inch apart in rows that are 12 to 14 inches apart. Once seedlings appear you can thin them to four inches apart.

The ideal soil temperature for carrots is 40 degrees Fahrenheit and they do best in neutral, sandy soil. Aim for a soil pH of 6.0 to 6.8. It is important to remove any stones from the area in which you plan to plant carrots, as they need to be able to easily push their roots through deep soil. The exception is when you plant the hardy Nantes carrot. Well-drained, loose soil can promote healthy root growth.

Avoid adding manure, as it can cause carrots to fork out and grow side roots. Adding a little bit of mulch can help promote germination and moisture retention. Be careful how much nitrogen is in the soil. Too much will make the tops grow great, but not the bottoms. Carrots do better with more phosphorus and potassium.

It is best to plant carrots three to four inches apart in rows that are twelve inches apart. You should give them one inch of water per week and fertilize them five weeks after you start them. It is important to weed around carrots thoroughly.

Cauliflower

There are two primary versions of cauliflower: white and orange. White cauliflower is the kind you commonly see in the supermarket with white budding heads. Some variations of white cauliflower include **White Cloud,** which is best known for being able to withstand cold weather and **Early White Hybrid** which is best known for its rapid maturity rate.

Orange cauliflower is similar to white cauliflower except for the fact that the buds are orange, due to their production of beta-carotene. Most commonly known as **Cheddar**, orange cauliflower grows just like white cauliflower. Its distinct feature is that you can space out its harvest.

Cauliflower, a distant relative of cabbage, is a tricky vegetable to grow because of its weather requirement and is therefore usually grown by professionals. However, if you have the right conditions, you can grow these in your own garden. The best time to begin planting cauliflower is one week before to one week after the last frost of the Spring. I recommend starting them indoors, six to eight weeks before you plant them outside. Cauliflower needs six hours of full sun exposure.

Cauliflower is another cool weather crop that does better in spring or fall. Mulch plants to keep roots cool and moist. The ideal soil temperature for cauliflower is between 60 to 70 degrees Fahrenheit in loamy, slightly acidic to neutral soil. The ideal pH of soil for cauliflower should be around 6.6. Cauliflower is best planted in soil that has been richly fertilized with organic matter. You can add some compost to the soil before you plant it as well. Cauliflower seeds are best planted eighteen to twenty four inches apart in rows. Rows should be thirty inches apart.

Well-fertilized soil can prevent cauliflower heads from buttoning. Side-dressing cauliflower with a nitrogen-based fertilizer can be helpful. Feed monthly with a commercial fish emulsion or make compost tea by soaking your homemade compost in a gallon of water for a few days. It is best to provide cauliflower with one to one and a half inches of water each week. It is important for cauliflower to have uninterrupted growth to develop successfully.

Celery

There are three main varieties of celery:

- **Leaf** – Leaf celery develops a thin stalk and big leaves.

- **Celeriac** – Celeriac celery develops a large root which can be eaten and is best grown in coastal areas. It can take between one hundred and one hundred and twenty days for this variety to grow.

- **Celery** – Plain old celery develops the big and crunchy stalks like the ones you can buy in the supermarket.

Celery is another tricky, long-season crop. It likes mild temperatures and generous moisture and it requires lots of fertilizer. The best time to begin planting celery is indoors, six to eight weeks before the last frost of the spring. You can soak celery seeds one day before planting to help boost the germination process. Celery requires partial to full sun exposure. The ideal soil temperature for celery is between 60 and 70 degrees Fahrenheit in any type of neutral soil. Celery does not grow well in cold weather.

Before converting celery from indoors to outdoors, add organic matter and compost to the garden soil. Celery seeds are best planted ten to twelve inches apart from each other and a quarter of an inch deep. You should mulch and water celery seeds directly after you transplant them and water them regularly. Without enough water, celery stalks can come out small and dry. Mulch and compost can help celery retain soil moisture. You can also tie the stalks together to prevent sprawling.

Corn

Corn is an annual. It is a wind-pollinated vegetable that grows with white, yellow or bi-colored ears. There are three main types of corn:

- **Standard Corn** – Standard corn is just as it sounds…the standard corn everybody is familiar with.

- **Sugary Enhanced Corn** – Sugary Enhanced corn is a hybrid variety with a sweet flavor. For most effective growth, this type of corn requires soil that is ten degrees warmer than that needed by standard corn.

- **Super Sweet Corn** – Super Sweet corn is another hybrid variety that provides the most sweetness. The minimum soil temperature for growing super sweet corn is 65 degrees Fahrenheit.

There are several different varieties that belong to each category of corn:

- Butter and Sugar: Standard corn, bicolor kernels, grows seven to eight inches within 73 days

- Jubilee: Standard corn, yellow kernels, grows eight to nine inches within 83 days

- Silver Queen: Standard corn, white kernels, grows eight to nine inches long within 88 days

- Concord: Sugary enhanced, bicolor kernels, grows six to eight inches long with a very early harvest

- How Sweet It Is: Sugary enhanced, white kernels, grows two ears per stalk within 87 days

- Kandy Korn: Sugary enhanced, yellow kernels, grows eight inches long within 89 days

- Early Xtra Sweet: Super sweet, yellow kernels, grows seven to nine inches long within 71 days

- Super Sweet Jubilee: Super sweet, yellow kernels, high yield

If you do not have a good deal of room in your garden, it is better not to plant corn. The best time to begin planting corn is two weeks after the last frost of the spring. Corn requires full sun exposure and it is better to plant in blocks rather than rows.

Block planting allows the pollen, found in the silk of the corn, to be easily blown by the wind or taken by beneficial insects to nearby stalks in order to ensure you get corn kernels on your ears. The best blocks are at least three rows wide. Corn is best planted five to seven inches apart and one inch deep. Blocks should be positioned thirty to thirty six inches apart. Weeding around corn is important but you can easily damage the roots so you must take caution.

The ideal soil temperature for corn ranges between 46 and 50 degrees Fahrenheit in well-drained, loamy and neutral soil. Corn is very tricky about its soil. For the best results, you can add compost or aged manure to the soil during the fall and let it sit throughout the winter. Before planting corn, dig in at least six inches of compost to the area because it is a voracious feeder of nitrogen. A side dressing of fish emulsion every month is beneficial to ear production. The Native Americans used to plant seeds in a mound with a fish placed on the bottom.

Corn does not fare well in cold weather. It is best to fertilize corn at the time of planting. You should also water it at that time and then again when tassels begin to appear. In dry conditions, you can water corn as much as five gallons per square yard.

Cucumbers

There are four main varieties of cucumber:

- **Slicing Cucumbers** – Slicing cucumbers are the long green kind you commonly see in the supermarket.

- **Pickling Cucumbers** – Pickling cucumbers are short, fat cucumbers with a dry skin.

- **Specialty Cucumbers** – Specialty cucumbers include all of the different sub-varieties of cucumber, such as "Lemon," and "Sweet Armenian."

- **Container Cucumbers** – Container cucumbers develop small vines and are good for growing in small gardens or containers.

The best time to begin planting cucumbers is one to two weeks after the last frost of the spring or if starting indoors, two to four weeks before planting outside. You can plant cucumbers one inch deep into the soil in rows that are six to ten inches apart. If you're starting them indoors, plant them twelve inches apart. Add compost or manure to the planting site before you add the seeds.

Cucumbers require full sun exposure. The ideal soil temperature for cucumbers ranges between 65 and 70 degrees Fahrenheit in loamy, neutral soil. Cucumbers require moist and well-drained soil. They do not fare well in cold weather at all and can easily experience frost damage.

You should frequently water cucumbers, once the seedlings emerge; as soon as the fruit begins to form you should water them with a gallon of water per week. Cucumbers need a great deal of nitrogen, so use compost liberally. You can use compost to side-dress the plants as the cucumbers are forming. If you use store-bought fertilizer during planting, ensure that it has a balance of low nitrogen to high potassium. You will also want to fertilize one week after the bloom, and then every three weeks thereafter. Since cucumbers are a climbing plant, you can use a trellis to help them grow upwards and to keep the vegetables off the ground.

Lettuce

There are 11 varieties of lettuce, making it one of the most diverse vegetables in existence. The varieties are:

- **Arugula** – Lettuce with long, spiky leaves often used in salads

- **Butter Lettuce** – Crispy head lettuce that is less compact than iceberg but has a tender texture

- **Little Gems** – Soft lettuce with a slight crunch

- **Mesclun** – Mixed lettuce

- **Mizuna** – An Asian variety of lettuce with long, spiky leaves similar to Arugula with a spicy twist.

- **Lambs' Lettuce** – Small bunches of dark green leaves

- **Oak Leaf Lettuce** – Loose leaf lettuce that can grow in green, red or bronze. Often used in salads

- **Purslane** – Commonly foraged and grows thick leaves

- **Romaine** – One of the most popular types of lettuce with thick, crunchy leaves

- **Watercress** – Lettuce with a slightly spicy flavor, often used in salads

- **Iceberg** – The most common type of lettuce, grown in tightly compacted heads with a watery flavor

The best time to plant lettuce is one week before to two weeks after the last frost of the spring. Lettuce requires partial sun exposure. You can also plant them indoors four to six months beforehand. The ideal soil temperature for lettuce ranges between 40 and 75 degrees, Fahrenheit, in loamy, slightly acidic soil. Lettuce grows best in well-drained, well-tilled moist soil. Lettuce can withstand mildly cold weather. It is best to water lettuce once a week, but also water it any time you see wilting leaves. You can fertilize lettuce three weeks after you convert it from indoors to an outdoor environment. Since lettuce is all foliage, it requires a great deal of nitrogen to grow those green leaves. Use an inch or more of compost as a mulch under lettuce plants. This will cool the roots and provide additional nitrogen.

The type of lettuce you want to grow, determines the planting depth for the seeds. For leaf lettuce, plant seeds half an inch deep and four inches apart. For loose-headed lettuce, plant half an inch deep and eight inches apart. For firm-headed lettuce, plant seeds half an inch deep and sixteen inches apart.

You can plant all types of lettuce in rows . Rows should be twelve inches apart. If you're going to be growing garlic, it is a good idea to plant it near the lettuce because it helps prevent pests. You can also plant your lettuce near tomatoes and corn because of their tall leaves. The extra shade can prevent bolting. You may need to weed around lettuce but take care not to damage its shallow roots.

Onions

There are four main varieties of onion:

- **White** – White onions are white on the outside and have a mild flavor. They are commonly eaten raw or cooked. Sub-varieties of white onions include **Snow White Hybrid, White White** and **White Granex.**

- **Yellow** – Yellow onions are yellow on the outside and white on the inside with a sweet flavor. They are commonly cooked. Popular sub-varieties include **Candy Hybrid, Walla Walla Sweet** and **Texas Super sweet.**

- **Red** – Red onions are red on the outside, red and white on the inside and are often eaten raw. Sub-varieties of the red onion include **Giant Red Hamburger, Salad Red** and **Red Delicious.**

- **Bunching** - Bunching onions don't form a bulb but rather a long shape such as green onions and scallions. Sub-varieties of bunching onions include **Evergreen Long White, Parade,** and **White Libson.**

The best time to plant onions is four weeks before the last frost of the spring. Onions require full sun exposure. The ideal soil temperature for onions ranges from 34 to 36 degrees Fahrenheit in loamy, neutral soil. Onions need well-drained and loose soil with a high level of nitrogen. Onions can easily withstand cold weather.

Before planting the seeds, you can add aged manure to the soil to help generate more nutrients. When you go to add the seeds in the ground, you can plant them one inch deep, five inches apart in rows that are twelve to eighteen inches apart.

It is best to add in high nitrogen fertilizer when you first plant the onions and then side dress the plants every couple of weeks until bulbs form. You can give onions one inch of water per week and use mulch to help them retain soil moisture. Add more water to get sweeter onions.

Parsnips

There are many different kinds of parsnip to choose from:

- **Harris Model** – This type of parsnip has sweet, white skin and straight roots that will grow within 130 days. The Harris model requires partial sun and consistent watering.

- **All American** – This type of parsnip grows rapidly and produces sweet skin. It requires partial sun and light watering.

- **Hollow Crown** – This parsnip variety grows long roots so you will need to till the soil deeply. Hollow crown grows best in acidic soil with consistent watering.

- **Cobham Marrow** – This type of parsnip grows roots that are up to eight inches long and it tastes very sweet. You must till the soil deeply to grow this variety.

- **The Student** – This type of parsnip can grow a thirty inch long root if the soil is tilled deeply enough. The student is a sweet and mild parsnip that requires partial sun and consistent watering.

The best time to plant parsnips is up to three weeks before the last Spring frost. Parsnips require partial to full sun exposure. Their ideal soil temperature ranges from 55 to 70 degrees, Fahrenheit, in loamy or sandy, acidic to neutral soil. When preparing to plant parsnips, you can dig fifteen inches into the soil, add in four inches of compost and then sow two seeds half an inch deep for every inch planted. Parsnips can easily withstand cold weather.

Always use fresh seeds when sowing parsnips. You should water them regularly throughout the summer if there is little to no rainfall. It is also important to weed around parsnips thoroughly.

Peas

There are three main varieties of peas:

- **Garden Peas** – Garden peas are the traditional variety that grow in an inedible pod. There are many sub-varieties of garden peas, including:

- **Spring** – Grows within sixty days, sweet flavor, six to seven peas per pod

- **Garden Sweet** – Grows within seventy five days, extra sweet, nine to ten peas per pod

- **Mr. Big** – Grows within sixty days, big dark green pods, nine to ten large peas per pod

- **Snow Peas** – Tiny peas with flat pods that are edible and sweet. Snow peas can be eaten raw or cooked. There are many sub-varieties of snow peas, including:

  - **Snowbird** – Grows within 60 days, short and sweet, two to three pods per plant

  - **Sugar Daddy** – Grows within 75 days, grows two feet tall, sweet pods

  - **Avalanche** – Grows within 60 days, six inch long dark green pods, grows three feet tall, sweet pods

- **Snap Peas** – Snap peas are round, fat and sweet with an edible pod and can be cooked or eaten raw. There are many sub-varieties of snap peas, including:

  - **Sugar Snap** – Extremely sweet, three inch pods, can grow up to six feet tall

  - **Sugar Bon** – Grows within 60 days, extremely sweet, three inch pods, can grow up to two feet tall

  - **Sugar Snappy** – Grows within 65 days, extremely sweet, crisp and large pods, can grow five to six feet tall

The best time to plant peas is four to five weeks before the last frost of the spring. Peas require partial to full sun exposure. The ideal soil temperature for peas ranges from 34 to 36 degrees Fahrenheit in loamy, neutral soil. Peas can easily withstand cold weather.

You can plant pea seeds once inch deep and two inches apart. Sometimes seeds will poke back out but you can push them back into the ground with a long, narrow object such as a chopstick. Before planting the seeds, you can add some manure and mulch to the soil. For good results, add wood ashes to well-drained soil prior to planting as well. Be careful not to add too much fertilizer to peas, as they are very sensitive to nitrogen.

The roots of peas like to stay cool, so be sure to mulch with straw or bark, but avoid compost mulch as it is nitrogen-heavy and will produce vines like crazy, but few peas. Peas tend to like bone meal, which is the best type of fertilizer to use on them. You can water pea plants sparsely.

Peppers

Since peppers come in many shapes, sizes, and colors there are actually thousands of different varieties of around the world! The most common sub-types of pepper are **sweet peppers** and **hot peppers.**

- **Sweet Peppers** - Sweet peppers are sweet-tasting, as their name suggests, and are commonly found in green, orange, red or yellow colors. They are often roasted or grilled and may be found in a wide variety of dishes. Some versions of sweet pepper include:

    - **Italian Frying Pepper** – skinny with a mild taste, commonly used in fried dishes

    - **Orange Bell Pepper** – orange in color, sweet, but not as flavorful as **the** red and yellow, often eaten raw or roasted.

    - **Purple Bell Pepper** –Purple in color, less sweet than their colorful counterparts but more sweet than the green. Purple bell peppers are often eaten raw.

    - **Red Bell Pepper** –the most common of the sweet peppers. Red in color, they are often roasted.

    - **Yellow Bell Pepper** – carry a mild taste compared to the red and orange varieties, but are great for roasting

- **Hot Peppers** – Hot peppers are less sweet and have a spicy kick. There are many common sub varieties of hot pepper, including:

    - **Jalapeno Pepper** – These peppers are the most common type of hot pepper. They are hot and spicy but not too fiery. Jalapeno peppers are commonly red or green and measure two to three inches in length.

    - **Cayenne Pepper** – These peppers often come red and dried out so **they** can be used as pepper. Cayenne peppers are hotter than jalapeno peppers and are believed to have healing properties.

- **Tabasco Pepper** – These peppers are green, red, yellow or orange in color and are used to make tabasco sauce. Tabasco peppers are much hotter than jalapeno and cayenne peppers.

- **Habanero Chili Pepper** – Habanero chili peppers have a **reputation** for being the hottest chili peppers of them all. This small pepper, usually green, yellow or pink in color, measures three centimeters in length.

- **Ghost Pepper** – The ghost pepper is the only pepper that is hotter than the habanero chili pepper. It can leave a burning sensation in your mouth for up to half an hour.

The best time to plant peppers is indoors, eight to ten weeks before the last frost of the spring. They can take up to three weeks to germinate. Peppers require full sun exposure. You can prepare the soil by adding manure, compost and fertilizer one week before you plant the seeds.

Plant peppers eighteen to twenty four inches apart in rows that are spaced twenty four to thirty six inches apart. The ideal soil temperature for peppers ranges from 70 to 80 degrees Fahrenheit, in loamy neutral soil. Peppers do not fare well in cold weather. Unless you live in a climate with extreme heat, one to two inches of water per week will be adequate.

You can fertilize peppers again after the fruits begin to appear. Once the peppers form you can use a fertilizer that contains plenty of potassium and phosphorous. Adding mulch to them can help manage weed growth.

Use Epsom salts on bell peppers to thicken the walls and make them juicy and delicious. Just dissolve two tablespoons Epsom Salt in a gallon of water and put some in a spray bottle. Spray the actual pepper with it at least once a week. Epsom salts contain magnesium, which thickens the wall of the pepper nicely.

Potatoes
There are hundreds of strains of potato, but they are divided roughly into seven main categories:

- **Russet** – Russets are medium to large sized oval-shaped potatoes with brown skin and a yellow interior. These potatoes have a mild flavor and are often used for baking.

- **Red** – These are small to medium, round in shape, and have red skin with white inside. These potatoes have a sweet to mild flavor and are often used in salads and soups.

- **White** – White potatoes are small to medium round potatoes with white skin and a white inside. They have a sweet to mild flavor and are often used for mashing, steaming and frying.

- **Yellow** – Yellow potatoes can range in size from a marble to the size of baking potatoes and grows in a round or oval shape. Yellow potatoes have a sweet and buttery flavor and are often used for grilling, roasting or in salads.

- **Purple or Blue** – Purple or blue potatoes are small to medium oblong vegetables with purple or blue skin and a purple or white interior. These potatoes have a nutty flavor and are often used for roasting, grilling or in salads.

- **Fingerling** – Fingerling potatoes are finger-shaped potatoes, two to four inches in length, that come in a multitude of colors including orange, purple and red. These potatoes have a buttery, nutty taste and are commonly pan-fried.

- **Petite** – Petite potatoes are literally bite-sized and they come in the same colors and flavor as fingerlings. These potatoes are often used in salads and for roasting and frying.

The best types of potatoes to plant are seed potatoes because they are less prone to diseases. Most garden centers sell certified seed potatoes that can give you great yields. One week before you plant the potatoes, put them in a warm area (between 60 and 70 degrees Fahrenheit) with plenty of light exposure to induce sprouting. A couple of days before you plant them cut the potato into pieces that contain two buds. Cutting the potato allows them to develop a thick skin that can protect them against rot.

The best time to plant potatoes is up to two weeks before the last frost of the spring. Potatoes require full sun exposure and soil that is well drained. If your garden has poor drainage, you can easily solve this problem by planting potatoes on raised beds. You should plant the starts three to four inches deep and nine to twelve inches apart. Rows of potatoes should be spaced thirty to thirty six inches apart.

Gophers love potatoes and sometimes will eat an entire crop before you even know it. Because of this, I plant potatoes in a tire tower. I stacked two tires on top of one another and filled the center with soil. I planted potatoes inside the tire hole and once the vines grew above the tire, I added another tire and put soil on top of the vines, but did not cover them. I kept doing this for about three more tires.

Once the plants blossom and mature just knock off a tire and harvest the potatoes, then another tire and so on. There is some controversy about planting food crops in tires, but I saw no adverse effects and the gophers did not get to them either.

The ideal soil temperature for potatoes ranges from 55 to 70 degrees, Fahrenheit, in sandy, acidic soil. Aim for a pH of 4.8 to 5.8. Potatoes can withstand mildly cold weather. You will want to water consistently when tubers begin to form, providing one inch of water per week. You can fertilize potatoes when they begin to bloom.

Pumpkins

There are tons of pumpkin strains. They grow in a variety of shapes and colors. Some of the most popular varieties include:

- **Aladdin** – Grows into a large, round pumpkin
- **Baby Boo** – Will yield small white pumpkins
- **Hooligan** – Yields tiny, light yellow pumpkins
- **Howden** – Produces a large, round orange pumpkin with a thick, upright stem
- **Iron Man** – Yields cannonball-shaped pumpkins with a bright orange color
- **Lumina** – Grows a pumpkin that is white on the outside and orange on the inside

The best time to plant pumpkins is one week after the last frost of the spring. Pumpkins require full sun exposure and plenty of space to grow their sprawling vines. You can also plant them indoors, two to three weeks beforehand, although they grow better when you plant them directly in the ground. If there isn't enough room in your garden, you can always plant pumpkins around the edges and direct the vines to grow away from the garden.

Pumpkins are best grown in hills, which can help the soil warm up more rapidly. You can prepare hills by loosening the soil and then digging manure into the ground. You can plant pumpkin seeds one inch deep, with three to four seeds per hill. Hills should be spaced at least four feet apart but no more than eight feet of separation. When the pumpkin plants begin to form you can thin them to two or three plants per hill.

The ideal soil temperature for pumpkins ranges from 55 to 60 degrees Fahrenheit. They will grow well in any type of soil, but they do not fare well in cold weather. Pumpkins grow best in moist, rich soil with plenty of compost and manure. Since they are heavy feeders you should add compost and manure regularly. It is best to water pumpkins with one inch of water per week.

Radishes

Radishes come in three main varieties:

- **Cherry Belle** – This type of radish has short tops, a crispy white skin and cherry-shaped roots.

- **White Icicle** – This radish can grow between five and ten inches long and has white skin.

- **Daikon** – This white radish can grow up to eighteen inches long and three inches in diameter. Daikon radishes have a mild flavor.

The best time to plant radishes is one week before to one week after the last frost of the spring. Radishes require full sun exposure and soil that is well-drained. You should plant radishes half an inch to one inch deep and one inch apart. Rows of radishes should be twelve inches apart. Once seedlings begin to appear you can thin them to three inches apart to avoid overcrowding.

The ideal soil temperature for radishes ranges from 39 to 41 degrees Fahrenheit in any type of soil. Radishes can easily withstand cold weather. Fertilize before you plant and keep the soil moist throughout the season. It is best to water your radishes once a week.

Spinach

There are three categories of spinach:

- **Savoy** – Savoy spinach grows deeply crinkled leaves that grow productively and can withstand cold weather the best of all the spinach varieties. Two of the most popular varieties of Savoy spinach are **Regiment** and **Bloomsdale**.

- **Semi-Savoy** – Semi-Savoy spinach produces leaves that are not as crinkly as Savoy, but they are more resistant to diseases, making this a popular strain for home gardening. The most well known varieties of semi-savoy spinach are **Tyee, Catalina, Teton,** and **Indian Summer.**

- **Flat-Leafed** – Flat-leafed spinach produces, as its name implies, leaves that are flat and smooth. Most processed spinach comes from the flat-leafed form of the vegetable. The most popular varieties of flat-leafed spinach are **Space** and **Red Cardinal.**

The ideal time to plant spinach is four to six weeks before the last frost of the spring. Spinach requires full sun exposure and soil that is well-drained. About one week before you plant the seeds, add some aged manure to your planting site. You can plant spinach seeds half an inch to one inch deep and twelve seeds per row. Treat with a fish emulsion when new growth starts. This will enhance the development of the vegetable.

The ideal soil temperature for spinach ranges from 55 to 65 degrees Fahrenheit in loamy, neutral soil. Spinach can easily withstand cold weather. Only fertilize spinach if it is growing slowly or if the pH of the soil is off-neutral. Always space spinach plants far apart, because growing close together makes the plants more susceptible to diseases like powdery mildew. You can water spinach once a week.

Zucchini

Aside from the common long dark green zucchini, there are two other varieties, **golden zucchini** and **globe zucchini**. Golden zucchini comes with a taste that is much milder than the green. Globe zucchini grows in a round shape, and can expand up to three inches in diameter.

The best time to plant zucchini is one week after the last frost of the spring. You can also plant it indoors two to four weeks before the last frost of the spring. Zucchini requires complete sun exposure. Like pumpkins, zucchini are heavy feeders so it is helpful to add lots of manure and compost to the soil before you start planting. Zucchini is planted one inch deep and two to three feet apart.

The ideal soil temperature for zucchini ranges between 55 and 60 degrees Fahrenheit, in loamy soil. Zucchini does not do at all well in the cold. Add compost and organic material to your soil before you add the seeds, for the best growth.

Zucchini requires moist and well-drained soil. Mulch can protect the short roots of this plant and retain moisture. Zucchini needs at least one inch of water per week. It also helps to fertilize zucchini occasionally to ensure that the plants do not grow deformed.

Normally, you get enough zucchini from just a few plants that you have to beg people to take them off your hands, because they produce so prolifically. The only thing that can prevent a large harvest is problems with pollination. Zucchini and summer squash produce both male and female flowers. Male flowers grow on straight stems and female flowers have a bulge under the flower. If there are very few female flowers, you can take an artist's paintbrush and gather pollen from the male flowers to deposit deep within the female flower and ensure pollination.

Tomatoes

There are a multitude of tomato varieties. The main categories include:

- **Globe** – Includes Campari and Husky Gold tomatoes
- **Cherry** – Includes Sun Gold and Sugary
- **Beefsteak** – Includes Beefmaster, Goliath, and Cherokee Purple
- **Plum and Pear** – Includes Juliet, Yellow Pear, and Roma

The best time to plant tomatoes is indoors, six to eight weeks before the last frost of the spring. Tomatoes require full sun exposure. If you live in the north, your tomatoes need at least six hours of sun. If you live in the south, it is okay if the tomatoes experience some shade during the day. To prepare the soil for tomato plants it is important to remove all debris, including rocks and weeds, from the ground.

The ideal soil temperature for tomatoes is 50 to 55 degrees Fahrenheit in acidic, loamy soil. Aim for a pH of 6.2 to 6.8. Tomatoes do not fare well in cold weather. They grow best in well-drained soil with plenty of fertilizer and compost.

Be generous with watering for the first couple of days after moving the crops from indoors to outdoors. After the initial planting, you should water tomatoes with at least two inches of water per week. Add mulch five weeks after the initial planting to help the tomatoes retain moisture.

Tomatoes are notorious for being heavy feeders. When you use eggs, keep the eggshells, wash them and crush them. Sprinkle the eggshells around your tomato plants to add calcium to the soil. This will help stop blossom end rot, when the bottoms of the tomatoes turn black and inedible.

Chapter 7: Care and Feeding Of Organic Gardens

Once you've put your garden together, the next step is to maintain it so that you will be able to garden in this spot year after year. The care of a garden includes watering, weeding, managing pests, and producing healthy vegetables with fertilizer.

If you choose not to take care of your garden, all of your hard work in preparation can quickly fall apart. It can easily be overtaken by weeds, bugs, insects, disease and other forms of blight. Knowing how to maintain your garden can prevent all of these. The good news is that once you have established a solid gardening care routine, it won't take up much of your time.

A Note on Watering

Most vegetables need about one inch of rain per week. If they are heavy feeders, or consist mostly of water, they need more. Tomatoes, zucchini and cucumber are among the vegetables that require a great deal of water.

Use a rain gauge in your garden to measure the water supply. Go out and measure immediately after each rain so that you get an accurate reading, before the water in the gauge starts to evaporate. If you find that you need to supplement with tap water, measure how much you add by checking your rain gauge.

Preventing/Getting Rid of Weeds

Weeds are annoying and pesky plants that grow quickly and can take over your garden. If left untouched, weeds can have a devastating impact on your harvest. While you cannot prevent weeds completely, you can take preventative measures to minimize their presence in your garden.

There are two types of weeds: **annual weeds** and **perennial weeds**. Annual weeds spread by seed, sometimes on their own and sometimes carried by birds or other wildlife. Annual weeds will appear in your garden both in the warm and cool season. Luckily, annual weeds often have shallow roots which make it easy to remove them from your garden with your hands or a simple tool.

Perennial weeds spread by seed and roots. Perennial weeds are difficult to remove due to their deep roots, which must be completely removed in order to prevent regrowth. While it is possible to remove perennial weeds by hand, it is usually easiest to apply chemical solutions. The best time to remove weeds by hand is in the early spring after the ground has thawed out from the winter.

Here are some tips for handling weed growth and prevention in your garden:

1. Pulling weeds is the most popular and effective way to get rid of them, but this can be a grueling and time-consuming task. However, if you plan to consistently pull weeds then it's not as bad because you're tending to them every week. If you plan to use weed pulling as your method of weed control, I highly recommend investing in a kneeling pad or an ergonomic tool that can reduce the physical stresses on your body as you weed.

2. One common way for a weed to invade your garden is when it comes in with a new plant. When a pre-potted plant sits for too long it will often sprout a weed or two. If you transplant it into your garden without first inspecting for stray weeds, you open your garden to the risk of weed infestation.

3. Try not to cultivate or till your soil any more than necessary. Weed seeds reside naturally in untouched soil. Excessive cultivation and tilling can expose those seeds to sunlight and cause them to germinate. Of course, a little bit of cultivation is okay, especially when your soil needs special preparation.

4. Mulch is your best friend when it comes to weed prevention. Adding mulch to your garden can suffocate weed seeds that might be lying around while it keeps your soil cool and moist. The only drawback to using mulch it that it can kill seedlings of your plants that self-seed. To easily avoid this problem, wait until the spring to apply the mulch. This way you will visibly identify all seedlings.

5. Planting vegetables that produce large leaves can help prevent weeds because they will protect your garden from sun exposure. Good examples of large leafy vegetables include tomatoes, potatoes, pumpkins and zucchini.

6. Rotating your crops each year can help slow weed growth.

7. When harvesting your plants, try not to disturb the surrounding soil. Weed seeds can easily dig themselves into soil breaks and germinate.

8. Watering your weeds can make them easier to pull out by hand because the water will soften the soil. The best way to do this is to water the weeds or wait for it to rain and then let the wetness soak in for a few hours before pulling them out. When you use water to weaken the soil, you are more likely to be able to extract the entire root system.

9. If you are planting a new garden, till the soil twice before you begin planting. This can pull weed seeds up to the surface, where you can easily spot them when they begin to grow. As soon you see them growing, you

can destroy the weeds, preventing them from taking over your garden later on.

10. If weeds are a problem in your garden paths you can apply rock salt or borax to any cracks along the path. If you choose this strategy, remember to wear gloves and be keep away from any plants you don't want to kill.

11. A natural way to prevent weed seeds from germinating is to use landscape fabric on your garden. Landscape fabric allows the soil in your garden to be exposed to air, water and nutrients, but it keeps weed seeds away from the sunlight. You can easily cut holes in landscape fabric to let your plants grow while at the same time protecting them from weeds. Planting your vegetables on raised beds helps too, because you can easily place the landscape fabric on the paths in between the beds.

12. If you have weeds growing with no vegetable plants nearby, you can pour boiling water on the weeds to eradicate them.

13. Herbicides are the best chemical option, because they attack weeds while not affecting the surrounding plants. The best time to apply herbicide to your garden is before weed seeds have a chance to germinate, but this can often be hard to determine, especially for first time gardeners. While old gardening wisdom says to apply it when daffodils begin to emerge, the most practical solution is to log the date when you first start to see weeds appear and then, the following spring, apply the herbicide to the garden three weeks prior to that date.

Preventing And Removing Pests Organically

Another challenge to keeping up your garden is pests. Pests, usually little bugs that like to invade your garden, can wreak much devastation, regardless of your gardening expertise. Pests commonly disease the harvest, cause yellow patches in your grass, eat their way through leaves, and stunt plant growth. Since pests live outdoors it is very hard to get rid of them completely. However, there are steps you can take to reduce the pest population, using safe, organic methods.

Here are the most common garden pests, how to identify their presence, and steps for managing them:

Anthracnose

Anthracnose is a fungus that causes blight in trees such as dogwood, ash and willow. When infected, trees will show brown spots that make them look burnt To help manage an anthracnose infestation, you cut off any diseased tree branches and prune to ensure healthy air circulation.

Aphids

Aphids are small green, grey, or brown bugs that feed off the juice from plant leaves and stems. They cluster at the tips of leaves and on their stems. There are several natural ways to manage an aphid infestation. You can spray them away with a high-powered stream of water or you can attract ladybugs, which will eat the aphids.

Prevent the infection by using the companion planting method. placing onions, garlic or chives nearby will keep aphids away. Watch for yellowing and stunting of peas caused by the mosaic virus. Aphids are usually the culprit behind this virus. Use insecticidal soap to get rid of them.

Beetles

Beetles like to burrow into the flowers and eat the leaves of plants. There are many varieties of beetle that can find their way into your garden. You can identify a beetle infestation by looking for ragged-looking, chewed up leaves.

The best way to manage beetles is to either manually pick them off your leaves or to apply insecticide. For further management, you can look for and kill the beetle eggs that are affixed to the underside of leaves.

The cucumber beetle can decimate an entire crop. Ladybugs and green lacewings eat the eggs of the beetle and stop an infestation. You can purchase these beneficial insects at your local nursery.

Caterpillars

Caterpillars are small but long and furry bugs that will chew holes through the leaves of your plants. You can often catch caterpillars in the act of destroying foliage. The best way to manage caterpillars is to kill them one at a time by hand or to spray with insecticide.

Chinch Bugs

Chinch bugs are insects so tiny you can barely see them with the naked eye. However, you can easily spot a chinch bug infestation by inspecting your lawn for yellow patches, especially during dry spells. These patches are created when the bugs suck the juice out of blades of grass. The only way to manage a chinch bug infestation is to use an insecticide, which you must apply every three weeks.

Cutworms

Cutworms live just beneath the surface of the ground. they chew the base of your plants causing them to die. You can locate cutworms by searching underneath the soil near any damaged plants. You can also protect your plants from cutworms by placing two-inch tall cardboard collars around the stems.

Earworms

Earworms attack ears of corn by burrowing through the silk as it emerges. The moth lays eggs on the silk. To prevent this from happening mix up one tablespoon of vegetable oil, one tablespoon of Bacillus thuringiensis (Bt), and two squirts of dishwashing liquid in two gallons of water and pour the mixture into a spray bottle. Spray the ears before the silk starts to grow out and thereafter at least once every other day.

Grubs

Grubs are the larvae of beetles; they also live primarily underground. If you notice plants just completely disappearing or can see that your turf is damaged, you may be dealing with grubs. The best way to manage a grub infestation is to manage the beetle infestation. However, if you find that grubs are already a problem in your garden, you will need to use insecticide to get rid of them.

Leafhoppers

Leafhoppers are tiny, triangle-shaped bugs that can jump from plant to plant. You can identify a leafhopper infestation by looking for curled leaves with small black holes. To control the leafhoppers, first try hosing down your plants. If that doesn't cure the problem you can move on to an insecticide.

Leaf Miners

Leaf miners make white trails inside layers of leaves. They may also leave dark spots on leaf surfaces. The best way to manage a leaf miner infestation is to completely remove all infected leaves. Do not put these leaves into compost or you can re-infect your plants.

Leaf Miners are attracted to radishes. If you plant radishes near spinach or another crop affected by this insect, the bugs will eat the **radish leaves and leave the spinach alone**. These insects do not inhibit the underground growth of the radish.

Mealybugs

Mealybugs are small, white, and fuzzy bugs that create sticky clumps on all parts of your plants, weakening them. The easiest way to manage mealybugs is to wash your plants down with soapy water or alcohol.

Moles

Moles are mouse-like pests that tunnel underground and eat grubs and earthworms. The telltale indicator of moles is a tunnel. The best way to manage a mole infestation is to focus on controlling your grub and earthworm population. Alternatively, you can catch them in traps and manually remove them from your garden.

Slugs and Snails

Slugs and snails are mollusks that both leave slime trails in their wake as well as holes in leaves and stems. Since slugs and snails are easily visible to the human eye you can hand pick them out of your garden. You can also trap them by leaving a few cabbage leaves on the ground near your damaged plants. Slugs and snails will gather under the leaves. Simply lift the cabbage leaves every one or two days to find and remove them.

Control slugs and snails by sprinkling sand (from a sandbox) under the plant. It cuts their soft underside and they will stay away. Cut the bottoms out of paper coffee cups and slide the cups over the foliage of small plants. This will allow the plant to get water and sunlight, but it will keep snails, slugs, cutworms and other insects from getting to the stems. Remove them once the plants grow larger.

Slugs and snails are also controlled by pouring beer into a shallow dish no more than ½ inch higher than the soil. The critters go for the beer and drown. Slugs and snails are also destroyed by table salt. Sprinkle some in their path or directly on the creature and it will melt before your eyes.

Spider Mites

Spider mites can cause extreme damage to your garden. The best way to identify them is to look for small webs that are barely visible as well as any damage to your plants. Mites come in the black or red variety and are very small. They cause yellow stippling on leaves and are easily knocked off with a blast of water every day or so. The best way to manage spider mites is to spray your plants with water, since they prefer dry conditions. You will need to apply miticide to control an extensive infestation.

Spittlebugs

Spittlebugs cause small white bubbles to form on plant stems. Spittlebugs don't cause too much damage to your plants other than causing the bubbles so you can easily spray your plants down with water to manage them.

Whiteflies

White flies are small, white fly-like bugs that lay eggs on the underside of leaves as they suck the juice of out your plants. The best way to control white flies is to consistently spray off your plants and promote good air circulation. Alternatively, you can destroy any infected plants to prevent white flies from spreading.

Pests That Specialize

Within the group of common garden pests there are some specific pests that love to go after vegetables. In this section, you will discover which pests like to eat which vegetables and what you can do to control and manage them.

Colorado Potato Beetle – This type of beetle likes to go after potatoes, peppers and tomatoes. You can identify the Colorado potato beetle by looking for defoliated vegetable plants and groups of yellow eggs on the underside of the leaves. You can easily destroy potato beetle eggs by crushing them with your hand. You can also handpick adult beetles and kill them by dropping them in soapy water.

Bean Leaf Beetle/Mexican Bean Beetle – This type of beetle goes after all types of beans. It looks like an orange ladybug, but it can decimate a bean crop. It affects any type of bean, from green beans to any type of legume. They usually attack the leaves of the plant. They lay yellow clusters of eggs on bean leaves. You can identify the bean leaf beetle by looking for holes in the leaves, stunted plant growth and pod damage. You can easily control bean leaf beetle infestations by letting loose Pediobus wasps or by hand picking the beetles off the tops and undersides of the leaves and destroying egg clusters.

Cabbageworm - Cabbage is susceptible to cabbageworm. Watch for small white butterflies that produce caterpillars that will devour cabbage leaves. Use an organic remedy called Bacillus thuringiensis (Bt) and mix one tablespoon in one gallon of water. Pour this solution over your cabbage plants every five days when caterpillars are active.

Cucumber Beetles – This type of beetle likes to go after cucumbers, pumpkins, squash, and sometimes corn, beans and peas. You can identify cucumber beetles by looking for damaged leaves, wilted vines, scarred vegetables and girdled seedlings. You can easily prevent a cucumber beetle infestation by fertilizing your crops early to encourage healthy root growth. You should also immediately remove and destroy any damaged plants as soon as you find them to prevent these pests from spreading.

Cabbage Looper – This type of caterpillar moves in looping motions and will go after cabbage, broccoli, cauliflower and kale. You can identify cabbage loopers by looking for holes between the veins of plant leaves. Bad infestations of cabbage loopers can cause stunted growth in your vegetables. You can take preventative steps against cabbage loppers by keeping up on weeding and proactively monitoring your vegetables for eggs.

European Corn Borer – This type of caterpillar like to go after corn but they will sometimes attack beans, peppers and potatoes. You can identify European corn borers by looking at the leaves of your corn and inspecting them for eaten leaves. You can easily manage a European corn borer infestation by destroying your corn stalks after picking the vegetables and by clearing your garden of weeds and debris at the season's end to destroy any potential borer shelters.

Tomato Hornworms/Cutworm – This type of caterpillar goes after tomatoes, peppers and potatoes, often feeding on vegetables that have not yet ripened. The best way to identify tomato hornworms is to look for defoliation at the tops of your plants. The bigger the hornworm, the faster the defoliation of your plants. You can proactively prevent tomato hornworm infestations by tilling the soil at the season's end to turn up any worms so you can easily kill them. It also helps to keep your garden weeded.

This insect likes to make a meal of young tomato stems. If you plant transplants, place half a toilet paper tube around the tomato. First cut the tube in half lengthwise (about 2 to 2-1/2 inches), cut small slits from one end up ½ inch or so around the bottom of the tube and flatten the tube at that end. Plant that end underground and it will keep the worm away.

Squash Bug – Squash bugs are flat, winged pests that like to go after squash, pumpkins and sometimes cucumbers. You can identify squash bugs by looking for wilting vines and yellow spots on the leaves of the abovementioned vegetable plants.

You can easily manage a squash bug infestation by using sticky traps to catch them during cool nights. You can also proactively monitor plants for adults and handpick them but this can be challenging since they like to flee quickly.

Organic Methods to Repel Pests

1. **Floating Row Covers** – These types of covers are made of transparent, polyester material that prevents pests from getting at your plants while still allowing sunlight to shine in. Floating row covers are best used as temporary barriers when your plants are young. It is best to use lightweight covers during the summer to prevent trapping your plants in too much heat. These covers are sold by the yard so you can buy as much as you need and then cut it down to fit over your garden.

2. **Pheromone Traps** – Most pests give off pheromones, odors that attract the opposite gender. Pheromone traps imitate these odors and are used to attract pests. The only drawback to this type of trap is that it generally only attracts males. However, you can use them early in the season to get a good idea of what kind of pests you may be dealing with for the rest of the season.

3. **Sticky Traps** – Sticky traps are made with bright colors and sticky material. Pests are drawn to the bright colors and then stick to the traps. It is best to hang stick traps at plant height about every three feet.

4. **Insecticide Soap** – Insecticide soap is made up of fatty acids that eat away the skin of pests. You can easily spray this liquid soap directly onto pests but it only works until the soap dries. The drawback to using this soap is that it can damage the leaves of certain plants. The best way to determine whether this soap will damage your plants is to test spray it on a few leaves before you completely spray the whole plant.

5. **Oil Spray** – Oil spray can suffocate pests and kill their eggs when you apply it directly to them. You can use dormant oil spray to kill pests during dormant seasons and use light oil spray to kill them during the growing season. It is best to use oil spray on small areas of plants only.

6. **Bacillus Thuringiensis (BT)** – BT is a natural bacteria contained in the soil. When you apply BT to a plant and a pest begins to eat it, the pest will become poisoned, stop eating the plants and eventually die. The drawbacks to using BT are that it only works on larvae, each pest requires a different type to kill it, and it can inadvertently kill good pests that you want in your garden.

7. **Chicken Wire Fences** – Chicken wire fences can protect your vegetables from larger pests such as rabbits, groundhog and deer. An effective chicken wire fence should be eight feet tall and extend two feet underground.

8. **Housing for Insect Predators** – A great way to control and manage insects is to provide housing and shelter for animals that prey on these pests. Toads, snakes, birds and spiders all prey on small garden insects so you can welcome them in by including birdhouses, shrubbery, upside-down flower pots and other shelters.

9. **Ladybugs** – Ladybugs are amazingly beneficial to any garden because they feed on most insects. You can buy ladybugs in bulk and add them to your garden when you have an extreme pest infestation. Other beneficial insects include wasps, nematodes, lacewings, hover flies and praying mantises.

10. **Practice Crop Rotation** – Pests and insects will often lay eggs at the site of your vegetable plants. By practicing crop rotation, you can disturb the eggs and prevent nymph bugs from infecting your plants.

    Crop rotation is very important in organic gardening. Never plant the same thing in the same place year after year. If you plant tomatoes on one side of your garden one year, plant spinach and cucumbers in that area the next. The tomatoes may exhaust minerals on that side of the garden and you need to plant something that is not such a heavy feeder in their area the next time. Sometimes disease will pop up when planting the same thing in the same location year after year. If you rotate your crops, it confuses the pests or substances that cause the disease and will keep your plants disease and pest free the next year. The YouTube video, <u>Crop Rotation Made Simple</u> by GrowVeg will show you more about rotating your vegetables.

11. **Practice Companion Planting** – Companion planting of certain items can provide a natural defense against pests. Basil goes well with tomatoes and peppers, Borage is a good companion for tomatoes and cabbage. Chamomile and dill companion well with cabbage, onions and cucumbers and catnip works well alongside squash and cucumbers.

    Certain vegetables in themselves can serve as good companion plants. Radishes and onions are the top two vegetables that naturally deter pests. Finally, certain flowers such as marigolds and sunflowers can help keep pests away while brightening up the garden.

    More companion plants include:

    -Rosemary
    -Oregano
    -Chives
    -Garlic
    -Mint
    -Lavender

12. **Powdered Kelp Spray** – A solution made from kelp powder can nourish your plants and help keep beetles and aphids away. You can easily spray this solution on your plants once a week during high infestation periods.

13. **Baking Soda and Water Spray** – A solution made from a few teaspoons of baking soda and water can be a great preventive spray for keeping mildew and fungus off plants.

14. **Human Hair** – Larger mammals such as rabbits and squirrels are repelled by the scent of human hair. It can also break down into the soil well and provide nutrients to your crops. If you're having a problem with deer, you can hang mesh bags of human hair around your garden to scare them off. You can use your own hair clippings or ask your local barber shop to provide some for you.

15. **Lawn Gnomes/Garden Décor** – Décor such as scarecrows, garden ornaments, lawn gnomes, wind chimes and the like can naturally repel larger, skittish pests such as deer. You can also border your garden will

towering plants to prevent larger pests from even being able to see your garden.

16. **Beer** – Sprinkling a little bit of beer into a small container and leaving it in your garden can help you catch snails and slugs for up to three days at a time.

17. **End of Season Garden Clean Up** – Always clean up your garden at the season's end to avoid inviting in pests. Keeping old vines and plants and other vegetable debris in your gardening area can attract all types of pests and bacteria, which will most certainly come back to haunt your garden after the winter.

18. **Coffee Grounds** – Sprinkling coffee grounds in your garden not only adds nutrients and acidity to your soil but it can also repel a variety of pests, including troublesome cats. Starbucks is known to provide used grounds for gardening projects so it doesn't hurt to stop by your local store and inquire within.

19. **Simple Soap Spray** – A simple spray made from soap and water can often kill many types of insects on contact, especially beetles.

20. **Chemical Insecticides/Pesticides** – Chemical methods of controlling pests should only be used as a last resort, when you cannot manage an infestation with organic methods.

Fertilizing

Fertilizing your vegetables can help promote healthy growth and yield amazing vegetables. How much fertilizer you use depends on several factors including soil type, season and crop type. Most gardeners prefer to use organic fertilizer when they grow vegetables, especially when they plan on eating them. The best source of organic fertilizer is compost. Another organic source of fertilizer is nitrogen-producing plants. You can plant them in the Fall, then chop them up and work them into the soil before they blossom. If you choose to use mainstream fertilizers, you can apply them to your garden a couple of days prior to planting your garden or even after you plant.

Mulch can also help fertilize your garden. Mulching your vegetables can help retain moisture, combat weeds, retain temperature and promote the overall fertility of your garden. You can create organic mulch out of materials such as leaves, straw, compost, sawdust, etc.

Disease

One other thing that you will need to watch out for is **disease**. Vegetable gardens are prone to various fungi, bacteria, and viruses. Vegetable plants can catch a disease through an animal host, through the soil or via wind and water. If one of your vegetable plants fall victim to disease, it can have stunted growth, a lack of flowers or just completely die. If your plants are exposed to extremely high temperatures, too much humidity or a lack of nutrients, they are more likely to catch disease.

The most common vegetable plant diseases are:

- **Root Rot:** Root rot occurs when the roots of a plant die. This can happen due to a variety of causes. The most common cause is overwatering, which waterlogs the plant. Soil fungi can also cause roots to die. A systemic infection can cause a plant to die quickly and completely. A smaller infection can cause slow death via wilted leaves. Root rot is best prevented by creating favorable planting conditions, including adequate soil drainage.

- **Downy Mildew:** Downy mildew is a fungal disease that targets cucumbers and cantaloupe and can caused stunted growth, poor fruit development and possible death of the entire plant. You can spot this disease by looking for pale green spots on upper leaves and eventual white growth on the lower leaves. The blades of the leaves tend to curl and will often die.

    Downy mildew usually begins in the center of a row or hill of crops and expands outward. It is often spread by the wind, rain or by the clothes of gardeners themselves. It thrives in humid warmth. The best way to manage downy mildew is to grow vegetable strains that are genetically resistant to this disease.

    You can treat for downy mildew by mixing four tablespoons of baking soda with one gallon of water and spraying this solution on the leaves of the plant. Apply this every day.

- **Powdery Mildew:** Powdery mildew is another common fungal disease that will leave powdery mildew on the heads, stems and leaves of vegetable plants. The leaves get a white or gray powder on them and the leaf will curl, exposing the underside. While this disease generally doesn't affect the vegetables themselves it can have an impact on their flavor.

    The best way to prevent powdery mildew is to make sure your plants receive adequate sunlight and are planted in a well-drained area. Avoid overcrowding. You can also plant a genetically resistant strain of the vegetable.

    To treat powdery mildew, remove any affected leaves and dispose of them in the garbage – do not put them in the compost. Rake the ground under the plants to ensure that all mildew is removed; then put down a fresh layer of organic mulch. This will prevent any spores that may still be on the ground from splashing up on the leaves. Avoid watering with a sprinkler; instead use soaker hoses so the leaves will not get wet.

To add to this treatment, mix 1-part regular milk with two parts water in a spray bottle, and apply to the leaves.

- **Curly Top Virus:** The curly top virus targets tomatoes, beans and peppers and causes their leaves to wilt. The leaves of these plants will curl and can thicken, possibly turning yellow. It can also deform the developing vegetables. To differentiate between the curly top virus and a simple lack of water, soak the soil around the plant with water and check to see if it looks better the next morning. If the leaves have not perked up, then you are probably dealing with the virus.

  The curly top virus is carried by the beet leafhopper. To prevent infection plant your tomato, bean, and pepper plants in a little bit of shade, which will deflect beet leafhoppers.

- **Blossom End Rot:** Blossom end rot is a serious disease that commonly targets zucchini, tomatoes and peppers and causes a black decay at the bottom of the vegetable. This disease is not caused by any bacteria, virus or fungus but by a calcium deficiency in the vegetable itself. The best way to prevent blossom end rot is to ensure that your soil has a pH of 6.5 by incorporate nitrate nitrogen when you fertilize.

  If you see blossom end rot, which looks exactly like the end of the vegetable is rotting and turning black, put a few calcium-infused antacid tablets into the soil at the base of the plant. Water immediately so that it will start to soak into the soil.

Chapter 8: Harvesting Your Vegetables

When the time comes to harvest your vegetables, there are no scientific guidelines, but there are a few general rules of thumb that can help you determine the best time to pick. The most common rule is to harvest your vegetables right before they reach full maturity but it can really vary between each different crop. If you wait too long to harvest a vegetable, it can turn tough, lose its flavor, or otherwise begin to rot. In this chapter, I will show you what you need to look for when it comes time to pick the different vegetables in your garden.

Beans: Harvest before you can see the seeds bulge from the pods. The pods should be tender enough to break into two. Monitor your beans regularly to determine harvest time because they can easily turn tough.

Broccoli: Watch your broccoli for the buds to be the size of a match head. Do not let the heads bloom all the way.

Brussels Sprouts: Watch for your brussel sprouts to be one inch in diameter and then twist or cut the sprout off of the stem.

Cabbage: Softly squeeze each head. If it feels solid, then it is ready to harvest.

Carrots: Carrots require a little bit of experience to know when they're ready for harvest. Watch for the tops to break through the soil and judge by the diameter. The best way to really know if your carrots are ready per your preference is to pull one out of the ground.

Cauliflower: Cauliflower is best harvested when the head is full and the curds feel smooth. However, it is important to note that the cauliflower in your garden will not appear as large as the kind you buy in the store.

Corn: The best time to harvest corn is three weeks after silks appear. You can also pop one of the kernels and look for a white substance to come out.

Cucumbers: Look for firm and smooth fruits with cucumbers. Since there are many varieties of cucumber, the time it takes to harvest will vary; however, it is important to pick them while they are still young.

Head Lettuce: Softly squeeze each head; if it feels firm, then it is ready to be harvested.

Leaf Lettuce: You can harvest leaf lettuce when the plant itself has grown to be four inches tall.

Onions: Although you can harvest your onions at any stage in their development, they will have reached their full maturity when the tops yellow and soften. When this occurs, you can stomp down the tops to facilitate further ripening. Loosen the soil around the onions and wait a couple days before pulling them up to dry in the air.

Parsnips: Leave parsnips in the ground over the winter and harvest them in the spring for the best taste.

Peas: Watch the pods until they look and feel full. The best way to know if they are sweet enough for your liking is to do a taste test.

Potatoes: watch for the top of the plant to dry out and turn brown. Slowly dig from the outside in to extract them from the ground.

Pumpkins: To harvest pumpkins, first watch for them to turn either orange or white. The vines should begin to wither. Poke the skin of the pumpkin with your nail to ensure that it has hardened enough.

Radishes: Watch for the bulbs to appear above the soil. Radishes grow quickly and will be ready to harvest sooner than most vegetables.

Spinach: While you can harvest individual leaves throughout the season, you will want to cut off the entire plant before a flower stalk appears.

 Zucchini: Zucchini is best harvested while it's young and tender. You want to be able to poke through the skin with your nail.

Tomatoes: Watch for tomatoes to fully gain their color and feel slightly soft.

Vegetable Preservation

When you have a healthy vegetable garden it will often provide you with more fresh vegetables than you, or your friends and neighbors, need. However, you can easily resolve this "problem" by learning to preserve fresh vegetables for your to use year-round. Here are several easy methods for produce preservation.

The Freezing Method

Freezing is the easiest way to preserve perishable food and you can easily store many vegetables in your refrigerator or a cool basement. The only drawback to freezing is that most refrigerator freezers have limited space. If you have a stand-alone freezer, however, this may serve you well.

Step 1: Pick your vegetables at their peak harvest time and inspect them to ensure they are free of spots caused by disease or rot. Remove any bad parts and peel them if necessary. Chop the vegetables into pieces and rinse them off.

Step 2: Add water to a pot, wait for the water to boil and add in the vegetables. This is called blanching. Blanching helps remove the enzymes that make the vegetables go bad and it preserves their nutrients. The length of time for blanching varies by the type of vegetable. Check with the National Center for Home Food Preservation for a chart that will provide blanching times for each vegetable. When ready, use tongs, a spoon or a strainer to remove the vegetables and transfer them to a container of ice for instant cooling.

Step 3: Allow the vegetables to cool on the ice and then drain off any additional water using a strainer. Get the vegetables as dry as possible, then place them into freezer bags or plastic freezer containers. Put as many vegetables as you can into each container to minimize the amount of air present. You can then place the containers in your freezer and store them until you're ready to eat them.

The Drying Method

Step 1: Pick your vegetables at their peak maturity and remove any spots caused by disease or rot. Peel the vegetable, if applicable. Prepare the vegetables to your liking by cutting, slicing, or chopping them. This is the form in which they will be used later. Try to keep your pieces similar in size to promote even drying.

Step 2: Blanch the vegetables using the same directions from the freezing method.

Step 3: Decide how you will dry your vegetables. You can do this in your oven, in the sun or using a food dehydrator. Dry the vegetables at 130 to 140 degrees Fahrenheit, ensuring consistent air circulation. You will know the vegetables are dry enough when they are leathery, or hard and brittle. Allow them to cool before packing in containers for storing.

Step 4: Package your dried vegetables by placing them in an airtight container. You can use a glass jar, sealable plastic bags or metal cans. If you use a metal can, first put the vegetables in a plastic bag. Pack as many vegetables into the container as you can without damaging them. Individually pack the quantity you will use in one sitting, since they can't be stored again after you've opened them. Store these containers in a dark and dry area and use them within six to twelve months of drying.

The Canning Method

Canning is a popular method of food preservation because it prevents harmful bacteria from entering the jars and ruining your vegetables. To can vegetables, you will need a pressure canner, which can help achieve the high temperatures you'll need for this method to work. You'll also need canning jars, which are designed to seal to keep out bacteria. Finally, you will canning jar lids and bands to complete the sealing process.

Step 1: Fill the rack of your pressure canner with four inches of water. Place your lidded jars, filled with vegetables of your choice, into the canner and lock down the lid. Turn on the heat and allow the water inside to come to a boil. Allow steam from the boiling water to escape the vents for 10 minutes before closing the vents or covering them with a weighted gauge.

Step 2: Ensure that the vents are closed over or covered with a weighted gauge so that pressurization can occur. The pressure level for canning vegetables is usually ten pounds. Once this level has been reached, begin to time the processing, based on the requirements of the vegetable you're canning. To find out the specific times for each vegetable, look up appropriate canning recipes.

Step 3: Once the processing time is up, you can turn off the heat and let your canner cool down. Only after all of the pressure has escaped from the canner is it safe to remove the lid. Always remove the lid away from your face to avoid burns from escaping steam.

Step 4: Take the jars out of the canner and let them cool off. As the jars cool, the lids should seal, depressing the center in a tight vacuum. After the jars are at room temperature, test the seal by pressing down on each lid. If a lid pops back up when you release pressure, it has not sealed and you will need to repeat the canning process, using a different lid. Never reuse lids. You can then store the canned food until you are ready to use it.

If you are new to canning, SoCals Preps has created a great video on introducing beginners to canning, entitled [Pressure Canners 101 – A Canner is a Canner...NOT TRUE](#).

Chapter 9: Delicious Vegetarian Recipes

Now you've got tons of fresh vegetables and a solid handle on gardening, but what do you do with all you've grown? Here are some of the most popular recipes from my vegetarian cookbook, that utilize many of the vegetables we have discussed growing. Of course, vegetable recipes don't stop here; there are many recipes that utilize the fresh vegetables you can grow in your garden, so many that it would take millions of pages to list them all. For now, however, here are a few easy and delicious ones that will get you started:

Baked Sweet Potato Fries

Ingredients:

- 3 sweet potatoes
- 2 tablespoon olive oil
- cayenne pepper
- cinnamon
- salt

Preparation:

1. Preheat the oven to 425° Fahrenheit.
2. Peel the sweet potatoes and cut them into long strips.
3. Mix the spices and olive oil together to taste and cover the fries in this mixture.
4. Lay flat on a foil-covered baking sheet and bake for 25 minutes, turning over the fries after the first 12 minutes and checking for tenderness to determine when they are done.

Roasted and Spiced Garbanzo Beans

Ingredients:

- 1 cup of cooked garbanzo beans
- 1 1/2 tablespoon olive oil
- 1/4 teaspoon cinnamon powder

- 1/4 teaspoon cayenne pepper
- 1/2 teaspoon cumin
- 1/4 teaspoon salt

Preparation:

1. Heat the oven to 450° Fahrenheit.
2. Rinse, drain, and pat dry the garbanzo beans.
3. Combine the oil and spices in a bowl, then add the beans and mix well.
4. Spread the beans evenly on a baking sheet and bake for 30 to 45 minutes, until the beans are crispy.

Roasted Beet, Sweet Potato and Parsnip Salad with Citrus Dressing

Ingredients:

- 2 beets, halved and sliced thinly
- 1 sweet potato, halved and sliced thinly
- 1 parsnip, sliced thinly
- 1 tablespoon olive oil
- 1/2 teaspoon salt
- A sprinkling of black pepper
- mixed salad greens, such as arugula, endive, oak leaf, etc. The amount is up to you, but start with at least six cups.
- 1 leek, thinly sliced
- 2 avocados

For Dressing:

- 1 orange, juiced
- 2 tablespoon fresh minced ginger

- 1 teaspoon honey
- 1 tablespoon olive oil
- Dijon mustard, optional, to taste
- 1 teaspoon. white wine vinegar
- Salt and pepper to taste

Preparation:

1. Preheat the oven to 400° Fahrenheit and line a baking sheet with parchment paper.
2. Toss the cut-up beets, sweet potatoes and parsnips with the spiced olive oil mixture.
3. Spread the vegetables evenly on the baking sheet and bake for about 30 minutes, turning them occasionally. The vegetables are done when tender but not too brown.
4. While the vegetables are cooking, mix the salad dressing ingredients together.
5. Wash and dry the lettuce. As the end of the vegetable cooking time nears, cut up the leek and avocado and arrange atop of the lettuce. lay the cooked vegetables atop the salad. Finally, top with the salad dressing or serve it on the side.

Quinoa Stuffed Peppers

Ingredients:

- 1 cup onion, chopped
- 2 tablespoons. olive oil
- 1 tablespoon ground cumin
- 2 cloves garlic, minced
- 1 cup spinach or kale
- 1 small zucchini, chopped

- 2 plum tomatoes, chopped
- 1 fifteen-ounce can black beans, rinsed and drained
- 1 cup uncooked quinoa
- 1 carrot, minced
- 2-3 cups of grated cheese of your choice, Monterey jack or cheddar, recommended
- Salt and pepper
- 6 large bell peppers, halved lengthwise, with ribs removed

Preparation:

1. Rinse the quinoa and place it in a pot with 2 ½ cups of water.
2. Bring the water to a boil. Lower the heat and simmer until all the water is absorbed, approximately 15 minutes.
3. Preheat oven to 350°Fahrenheit.
4. Heat the oil in a saucepan over medium heat. Add the carrots and cook for five minutes, or until soft. Then add zucchini and garlic, cooking another two to three minutes.
5. Add tomatoes, cumin, and spinach or kale, then sauté for one minute, until wilted.
6. When the vegetable mixture and quinoa are done, stir everything together, including the black beans and 1 cup of the cheese. Add salt and pepper if needed.
7. Cover the bottom of the baking dish with a small amount of water.
8. Fill the bell peppers with the quinoa mix and set them in the baking pan. Cover the dish with aluminum foil and bake for one hour.
9. Uncover the baking dish, and sprinkle the remaining cheese on each pepper. Bake, uncovered, for an additional 15 minutes, until the cheese has browned.

Black Bean Veggie Burgers

Ingredients:

- 15 ounce fresh black beans
- 1/2 green pepper, minced
- 1 cup spinach, kale, or both, minced
- 1/2 white onion, minced
- 1/2 cup corn
- 2 cloves garlic, minced
- 1/4 cup parsley, minced
- 1/3 cup pumpkin seeds, chopped
- 1 egg
- 1 tablespoon cumin
- 1/2 tablespoon chili powder
- 1/4 teaspoon Cayenne
- 3/4 cup bread crumbs
- 4-6 whole grain buns with optional cheese, tomato and avocado

Preparation:

1. Preheat the oven to 375°Fahrenheit.
2. Rinse and drain the black beans. Mash the beans well.
3. In a separate bowl, mince the green pepper, onion, garlic, parsley, pumpkin seeds, and spinach or kale. Add in the corn and beans.
4. Mix the egg and spices together, then add the mix to the bean mixture. Finally, add in the bread crumbs, mixing well.
5. Form 4-6 patties, depending on the size of burger you prefer.
6. Place the patties on a parchment paper-lined baking sheet and bake for about 10-15 minutes. Flip the patties and bake another 10-15 minutes.

7. A great way to complement the burgers is to toast the buns and add cheese, tomato and avocado.

Sweet Potato Mac and Cheese

Ingredients:

- Whole wheat pasta of your favorite shape
- 3 tablespoon unsalted butter
- 3 tablespoon all-purpose flour
- 2 cups of milk, whole preferred
- 1 large sweet potato, cut into small cubes and cooked
- 2 cups shredded cheese, either a blend or cheddar
- Fresh sage, chopped
- Salt and pepper as needed

Preparation:

1. Preheat the oven to 350°Fahrenheit.
2. Peel and cut the sweet potato into small cubes. When the oven is hot enough, put the sweet potato cubes onto a baking sheet and cook for 30-45 minutes, until tender.
3. Meanwhile, bring a pot of water to a boil and cook the pasta.
4. In a sauce pan over medium low heat, melt the butter, but don't let it brown. Add the flour and whisk constantly for two to three minutes, turning down the heat if necessary.
5. Add the milk in a steady stream, stopping after one cup and continuing to whisk for two to three minutes. Add the second cup of milk, still whisking and cooking for another few minutes while it thickens. Add the salt and pepper.
6. Add in the cheese and stir until smooth. When the cheese mixture is ready, add the cheese, sweet potatoes, sage and pasta together and gently stir.

7. Depending on how crispy you like your mac n cheese, either put in a 9 by 13 or 8 by 8 inch dish and top with more cheese if desired. Bake for 25-30 minutes.

General Green Smoothie Recipe:

Ingredients:

- 1-2 cups of leafy greens, preferably kale, spinach, collards or chard.
- 2 fruits of your choice
- 1 vegetable, such as cucumber, carrot or celery
- 1-2 cups of liquid: water, milk, or fruit juice. The amount will depend on how much liquid you want in your smoothie and how much is needed to blend in the fruits and vegetables. It is generally best to use water for most healthy smoothies.

Preparation:

Let your smoothie blend for a few minutes so that it becomes creamy instead of lumpy. Using either frozen fruit or ice cubes in your smoothie will give it a thicker consistency.

Conclusion

I hope this book was able to help you to discover what you need to do right now in order for you to get started on planning, building, and producing a high quality vegetable garden that will give you years of health and pleasure while saving you money at the same time!

A vegetable garden can help you lower your grocery budget, sustain your physical health, and reduce your stress levels. There really are no big drawbacks to gardening, as long as you are willing to spend some time and a little money on it! With enough proper planning, you can be on your way to becoming an amazing gardener who can produce massive amounts of high quality and nutritious vegetables for less than half the price of what you'd pay in the store.

Organic vegetables are full of key ingredients that provide a whopping nutritional boost to your body. If you choose not to eat them fresh, or if you end up with so many that you simply *cannot* eat them fresh, you can preserve them by drying, freezing or canning them. This will allow you to enjoy the "fruits" of your labors in the off-season. However, my personal absolute favorite way to use up all the things that I grow is to use a masticating juicer, and juice it all. A masticating juicer tends to give more juice, taste fresher, and give more nutrients as well.

Your next step is to start thinking about what type of garden you want to grow, where you will place it, and what kinds of vegetables you wish to grow. I've included detailed information to help you select the most appropriate location for your garden. Remember that sun exposure is the most important factor to consider when planning a garden. Without enough sunlight, your vegetables may not sprout at all! Second only to sunlight, proper soil drainage is essential to prevent myriad problems from plaguing your garden.

It's also a good idea to figure out your pest control strategy before you start planting. This way, you'll already know what kinds of pests to look out for and you can take preventative measures to protect your garden from infestations before it's too late. In the event that an infestation occurs, you will be able to refer back to this book for specific steps to identify and eradicate any problems that may have arisen.

Go ahead and enjoy some of the flavorful recipes that were included in this book to whet your appetite and get you motivated for your delicious meals made with your own delicious vegetables. As your vegetables ripen in your garden, revisit these recipes and plan how to turn your veggies into delectable meals.

Finally, if you discovered at least one thing that has helped you or that you think would be beneficial to someone else, be sure to take a few seconds to easily post a quick positive review. As an author, your positive feedback is desperately needed. Your highly valuable five star reviews are like a river of golden joy flowing through a sunny forest of mighty trees and beautiful flowers! *To do your good deed in making the world a better place by helping others with your valuable insight, just leave a nice review.*

My Other Books and Audio Books
www.AcesEbooks.com

Health Books

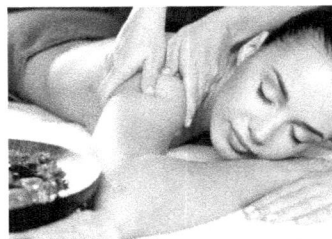
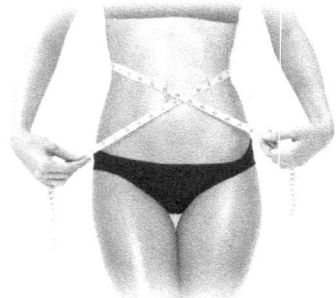

Peak Performance Books

Be sure to check out my audio books as well!

 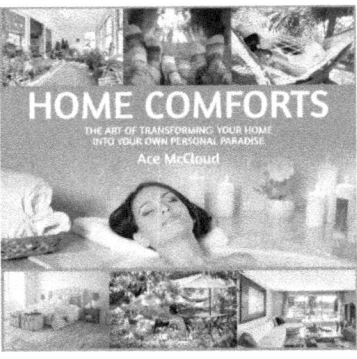 

Check out my website at: www.AcesEbooks.com for a complete list of all of my books and high quality audio books. I enjoy bringing you the best knowledge in the world and wish you the best in using this information to make your journey through life better and more enjoyable! **Best of luck to you!**

www.ingramcontent.com/pod-product-compliance
Lightning Source LLC
Chambersburg PA
CBHW051421070526
44584CB00023B/3529